is it just me or is
everything
great?

is it just me or is everything great?

Geoff Tibballs

MICHAEL O'MARA BOOKS LIMITED

First published in Great Britain in 2007 by
Michael O'Mara Books Limited
9 Lion Yard
Tremadoc Road
London SW4 7NQ

Copyright © Michael O'Mara Books Limited 2007

Illustrations © David Woodroffe 2007

A CIP catalogue record for this book is available from the British Library

ISBN: 978-1-84317-245-1

10 9 8 7 6 5 4 3 2 1

www.mombooks.com

Designed and typeset by Design 23

Printed and bound in Great Britain by Clays Ltd, St Ives plc

Papers used by Michael O'Mara Books are natural, recyclable
products made from wood grown in sustainable forests.
The manufacturing processes conform to the environmental
regulations of the country of origin.

INTRODUCTION

Why do we look at things in such a negative way? The cup is always half empty instead of half full. Yet for the price of a pair of rose-tinted spectacles everything can appear so much brighter. For example, you arrive home and find your partner in bed with a stranger. Don't look upon it as losing a wife, think of it as gaining a new friend. Similarly, if your house is razed to the ground, instead of seeing it as being made homeless, look on it as finally having got rid of that red flock wallpaper in the lounge. And if you have the misfortune to lose a leg in an accident, try to look on the bright side. You'll get weeks off work, lots of sympathy, free membership at a pogo club, and the chance to star in the forthcoming biopic of Heather Mills. By using more spin than Shane Warne, you can look positively at a whole range of issues. So cheer up and get out and smell the roses – even if you know it's really dog shit.

GEOFF TIBBALLS, 2007

ACCOUNTANTS

So maybe accountants are a little dull. Maybe it's true that the definition of an extrovert accountant is one who looks at *your* shoes while he's talking to you instead of his own, and that an accountant's idea of trashing a hotel room is refusing to fill out the guest comment card. But if you find a good accountant – particularly one who has a tax loophole named after him – he can be worth his weight in ledgers. In fact, provided you are willing to look beyond the chronic lack of charisma, accountants score a number of points in the credit column and are well worth befriending.

For example, inviting an accountant to your party will automatically make you appear more interesting by comparison, in the same way that George Bush looks intelligent next to his son and a penguin looks agile on dry land compared to a wardrobe. Accountants themselves try a similar tactic, which is why they invariably invite funeral directors to their parties. Also, you never know when a question on auditing is going to come up on *Who Wants To Be A Millionaire?* And whereas some women go for footballers or firemen, Carol Vorderman probably goes weak at the knees over accountants' chat-up lines.

ACCOUNTANT: Yours is the sort of figure I'd like to look

at all day, Carol.

CAROL: You saucy boy.

ACCOUNTANT: And you'd look good on my sheets – accounts sheets that is.

CAROL: Oh, you silver-tongued swine! Take me . . . now!

ADVOCAAT

Famously described by Alan Coren as a Dutch drink made from lawyers, advocaat is every aged aunt's favourite Christmas tipple. And that's why it's great, because that heady mix of egg yolks and brandy gives Aunt Aggie the nerve to mime 'The Stripper' at charades or heckle the Queen's Speech. Also, once you've tasted advocaat, you'll never have to drink anything as disgusting again – and that includes any product manufactured by Ronseal.

AIR KISSING

When two people greet each other by ostentatiously planting kisses in mid-air to the sound of 'Mwah', 'Mwah', it looks the daftest thing since the Monty Python fish-slapping dance. But air kissing does have certain advantages. It greatly reduces the risk of spreading germs, it conceals the fact that you've recently eaten copious amounts of garlic, your lipstick doesn't get smeared in a line across your face like a plume of vapour from a jet engine, you don't have to worry about where to put your nose, and you're not in danger of receiving an unexpected

and unwanted tongue down your throat. Air kissing is also a useful tool if her psychopathic husband recently released from jail is watching closely or if you're really interested in looking at her bum as opposed to her face. In fact, it could be said that those who indulge in air kissing are making something of a statement, the statement in question being: 'We're total prats.'

AIRPORTS

The phrase 'terminal illness' could first have been applied to airports. Two hours never passes so slowly as at an airport – unless, of course, one of your party has had to dash home for their passport. However, while it is true that they can be soulless places, airports do have their plus points.

- While your flight is delayed for seven hours, you can look at the departure board and see where everyone else is flying off to.
- You can visit the Duty Free shop and buy all manner of drinks and sweets that you don't really like. But at least you're getting a bargain. Maybe.
- You can watch your luggage being loaded by trained baggage handlers who treat your personal possessions the way Geoff Capes used to treat a shot put.
- The check-in clerk always greets you with a smile – but that's only because she has just seen your passport photo.
- If you're lucky, you'll get chosen for a free massage – or 'body search' as they prefer to call it.
- There's a good chance you'll appear on a TV docusoap.
- Unquestionably, an airport is the best place from which to catch a plane.

AMERICAN COURTESY

Some American platitudes can be harder to stomach than sheep's eyeballs in a warm vomit sauce. When your waitress says to you 'Enjoy!', it can really grate. You think to yourself, 'I don't need guidance. I know that the object is to enjoy the meal, thank you very much. That's why I'm paying an extortionate amount for it. But I promise you, if I don't enjoy it, you'll be the first to know.' Then there's the ubiquitous 'Have a nice day.' The people who blurt out that mindless rubbish, do they ever stop to think for a moment? They have no idea what your plans are for the day. You could be on your way to your father's funeral. How's that going to be a nice day? It's not as if the greeting is going to have a favourable effect on your fortunes. No doubt Custer's mother said 'Have a nice day, George' before he set off for the Battle of Little Bighorn.

But let's not be too harsh. At least American restaurant and shop staff do make an effort to be polite, which is something their British counterparts could never be accused of. In Britain, 'Enjoy!' is invariably replaced by a surly grunt that swiftly turns to downright hostility if you fail to reward their rudeness with an adequate tip. As for 'Have a nice day', stressed Londoners take the view that if they're not going to have a nice day, why should anyone else be allowed to? So a little courtesy, even if it is served with a side plate of insincerity, can do no harm, and if just one person actually has a nice day as a result, it will have been worthwhile . . . unless, of course, that person was on his way to rob a bank.

APATHY

Don't knock apathy. It's great. Maybe.

ARKANSAS

Arkansas pretty much epitomises that archetypal oxymoron, 'redneck culture'. Arkansas and its inhabitants (known none too affectionately as Arkies) are viewed as a standing joke by other American states. Even Mississippi looks down on Arkansas. Yet Arkansas has its own state bird (the mockingbird), state insect (European honey bee), state vegetable (the South Arkansas vine-ripe pink tomato) and state folk dance (the square dance). It is also home to such luminaries as John Grisham, Glen Campbell, John Daly, Johnny Cash, Billy Bob Thornton, Conway Twitty and Bill Clinton (okay, forget about Clinton). Besides, there are loads of good points to living in Arkansas:

- You know every line from *The Dukes of Hazzard*.
- Your dad can walk you to school because you're both in the same grade.
- Your dog can act as a dishwasher.
- Moving home is easy – your house is on wheels.
- All you need for formal occasions is a different baseball cap.
- Because your niece is also your wife, you save on birthday presents.
- You never need to pay for a haircut.
- You can tell your age by the number of rings in the bathtub.
- Foreplay simply consists of taking off her saddle.

ASTROLOGY

A lot of people dismiss astrology as a meaningless waste of time. Huh, typical Capricorns! But astrology is great because it gives you a ready excuse for whenever you foul things up. You can blame everything on fate because, contrary to popular belief, astrology is an exact science. Every word in your daily prediction could apply to you.

Or someone you know. Or someone else.

- 'Sorry, darling, I drove the car into a river. But it would have happened even if I hadn't accidentally put my foot on the accelerator instead of the brake. You see, my stars said that today was an important one for a water sign. I just didn't see it.'

- 'Sorry, darling, I ruined your best shirt with the iron. But it's not my fault. My stars said that today I shouldn't deal with anything pressing.'

- 'Sorry, darling, I embedded an axe in your mother's head this morning. It was bound to happen. My stars said that today I would suffer a complete nervous breakdown and turn homicidal around 10.45 a.m.'

ATHEISM

As I see it, the only problem with being an atheist is not knowing who to cry out to during orgasm. Otherwise atheists never have to buy new hats to wear in church, never have to watch *Songs of Praise*, never have to remember the names of Jacob's sons and never have to make cucumber sandwiches.

B

BALDNESS

If there's one thing guaranteed to give men sleepless nights, it's the dread of losing their hair. Most men would rather go through the pain of childbirth than discover a nest of follicles around the plughole after they've washed their hair. But why? Hair is perceived as a sign of virility but has anyone ever claimed that Boy George is more masculine than Ross Kemp? Or that wearing what looks suspiciously like a dead hamster on your head makes you irresistible to women? So ditch that toupee and dwell instead on the advantages enjoyed by bald people:

- You never have a bad hair day.
- You save a fortune on shampoo.
- You can be in and out of the hairdresser's during a commercial break on *Trisha*.
- You never have to remember where you've put your comb.
- Nobody tries to sell you expensive haircare products.
- You can sell your forehead as advertising space.
- You're never going to be mistaken for Russell Brand.
- You never have to worry about the length of your fringe.
- When aliens land on Earth, with whom are they going

to identify? Bald people. So slapheads will be the first to be invited on board the spaceship and will be the obvious choice to be elevated to high command in the new regime, to baldly go . . .

BANKS

Yes, they're greedy corporate bastards. Yes, they bombard you with loan applications and then crack down on you like the Russian Secret Police if you're £5 overdrawn for a day. Yes, they take an eternity to clear a cheque, allegedly to safeguard your security, but really so that they can line their own pockets in the meantime. Yes, many of their charges are immoral, if not illegal. But a bank is still a safer place to deposit a sizeable sum of money than any of the following:

- Under a mattress.
- In a biscuit tin.
- Down your underpants.
- With a heroin addict.
- On a grass verge.
- In a shredder.

BARBIE

Barbie has been charged with being materialistic simply because she constantly needs to replenish her wardrobe. She may have got through more than a million pairs of shoes since her birth in 1959, but she's no brainless

bimbo. Don't forget, she has been a doctor, a pilot, an astronaut, a TV news reporter, a business executive and an Olympic gold medallist. Imagine what she could have achieved if she'd had a boyfriend with balls.

KEN BARLOW

Coronation Street's resident intellectual is regularly mocked for being dull. Excuse me. The bloke's been married three times, had a number of affairs and countless girlfriends. That's not dreariness, it's exhaustion.

BATH FOAM (CHEAP)

It not only gives you a cut-price soak, it also removes any limescale from around the bath at the same time.

VICTORIA BECKHAM

I may be in the minority – OK, yes I am in the minority – but I admire Victoria Beckham. Considering she has never physically hurt anybody in her life, she should not have to put up with the amount of abuse and ridicule she receives. She is targeted over her weight, her singing, her clothes, her marriage, her intelligence, just about everything – and usually from people like Naomi Campbell or the truly abysmal Rebecca Loos. Unless he was secretly drugged beforehand, why would David Beckham even look twice at the Loos woman? It's like Paul Newman once said: 'Why fool about with hamburger when you can have steak at home?' Except that Rebecca Loos doesn't even qualify as hamburger – she's just scrag end. For let's not forget, Victoria was – and still is – a beautiful woman. She was certainly the best looking Spice Girl, although Mel C was not helped by being forced into unflattering clothes, which, as Jonathan Ross put it, made her look like a single mum on a council estate.

Victoria has treated most of her critics with the contempt they deserve and has fiercely defended her husband, but even then she is accused of being needy and desperate to hang on to the Beckham brand at all costs. Or could it simply be that she genuinely loves him? Even in the ghastly world of celebrity, these accidents do occasionally occur.

Victoria has been mercilessly mocked for reportedly saying, 'I've never read a book in my life.' However, the original interview appeared in a Spanish newspaper, and was conveniently misinterpreted. What she actually meant was that she never has time to finish reading a book because she is always running around after her children. Slightly different. Victoria is also deceptively witty. When Naomi Campbell rounded on her and asked cattily, 'Why do they call you Posh?' Victoria snapped back, 'Why do they call you beautiful?' It's a riposte worthy of Dorothy Parker, or at the very least, Lee Mack.

Her critics say that because she courts publicity, she has to accept the rough with the smooth. Fair point, but most wars do have the occasional ceasefire. It's just a shame that she broke her promise to give up singing in order to join the Spice Girls reunion. Or does that count?

BIN POLICE

Reports suggest there is currently an even greater threat to the world than bin Laden: bin police. Most of us are happy to do our bit to save the planet, but in some parts recycling has become a crusade with draconian measures taken against anyone who falls foul of the complicated rules and regulations. In 2006, singer Charlotte Church was ticked off by a crack member of Cardiff's Recycling Team for leaving a dozen bin bags outside her house on the wrong day and for failing to recycle. Cardiff Council explained: 'Residents are supposed to put general waste in a black bin, collected each week. Compostable materials go in a green bin, and plastic, tins and glass in green bags, which are taken away on alternate weeks.' It's that simple. Even allowing for grey areas concerning paper envelopes with cellophane windows and cartons that could be either plastic or cardboard, household recycling can only be a good thing.

For a start it has brought a new purpose to empty lives. The excitement as bin collection day approaches is almost tangible.

HUSBAND: Which bin has to go out tonight, dear?

WIFE: It's the brown one.

HUSBAND: Not the brown one with the grey lid?

WIFE: No, that's next week.

HUSBAND: What about the green one?

WIFE: No, that's only to be collected when there's a full moon.

HUSBAND: And remind me again, what goes in the black bin?

WIFE: Anyone from the recycling team I catch snooping around.

The diversity of collection means that we get extra exercise from wheeling the bins up the drive and it also affords the binmen the opportunity of scattering new types of refuse along your road. Whereas previously they had to content themselves with dropping the odd crisp bag, now they can leave behind them a trail of assorted rubbish. It must make their job all the more rewarding.

BLACK WIDOW SPIDERS

So many women are terrified of spiders. Why? The female black widow spider could be a role model for women. She gets to kill the male immediately after mating, which, apart from anything else, stops the snoring before it even starts.

DAVID BLAINE

People are always having a dig at David Blaine, but if he weren't around, somebody else would have to be the most pretentious prat in the world.

BLAME CULTURE

That there is something undignified, almost dishonest, about trying to attach blame following a personal tragedy is an attitude encouraged usually by those who were at fault. If someone dies as a result of a hospital's negligence, why shouldn't that hospital be held accountable? Who else was to blame? The fairies? The previous government? The Man from Del Monte? But to listen to hospital administrators ('terrible tragedy', 'heartfelt condolences', 'you're not getting a penny out of us'), the victim's family should simply move on and forget all about any form of financial compensation. And if they do press for compensation, it is hinted that they are being greedy and are somehow sullying the victim's memory. Something about pot, kettle and black springs to mind.

JAMES BLUNT

Why does everyone hate James Blunt? A recent survey named him as the fourth most annoying thing in the UK, beaten only by cold callers, queue-jumpers and caravans. This made him more irritating than traffic wardens, tax returns, mosquitoes or diarrhoea. The derogatory term 'He's a right James Blunt' has now entered Cockney rhyming slang while Paul Weller declared that he would rather eat his own excrement than duet with Blunt. Another critic wrote: 'James Blunt is so annoying he makes me want to rip my eyeballs out just to have something to plug my ears with.' Even Alastair Campbell would be hard pushed to turn that into a positive review.

So why the hostility? What has Blunt done to offend so many? Has he been caught robbing charity boxes? Has he been a character witness for Heather Mills? Did he poison Desert Orchid? No, his biggest crime seems to have been to have an affair (allegedly) with Tara Palmer-Tomkinson, which merely calls into question his mental state and suggests that the ex-soldier was suffering from something similar to Gulf War Syndrome.

Unlike Pete Doherty, a hero to dozens, even though his talent remains a closely guarded secret, Blunt has never been to jail and doesn't do drugs. He has also fought for his country. True, his girlie voice is not one that would normally be associated with army life (hinting that the former captain got his privates caught), but it is suited to his songs. He has won two Ivor Novello awards for songwriting, and Elton John chose 'You're Beautiful' to be played at his wedding to David Furnish. While you wouldn't trust Elton with your wardrobe, he can spot a decent tune. Meanwhile, Blunt's 'Goodbye My Lover' has become one of the most popular songs to be played at funerals, which is why people say, 'You'll play James Blunt over my dead body!' In 2006 it was reported that a six-year-old girl woke from a coma after hearing 'You're Beautiful', although some say it was listening to James Blunt that put her in a coma in the first place. Others claim that Blunt's songs are shallow, but, in an impassioned defence of the singer in the *Daily Mail* (well, he's not an asylum seeker), Sarah Sands went all Basil Fawlty as she pointed out: 'These are pop songs, for goodness sake – what do you want to find underneath them? The Gettysburg Address?'

Precisely. The truth is that Blunt-baiting has become a disturbing national trend, like binge drinking and *Strictly Come Dancing*. It's time to call a truce and wave the white flag, which brings me to another persecuted species, the Dido . . .

BOTTLE BLONDES

Bottle blondes are like airplanes: they're fast, it is often a bumpy ride and the most sought-after piece of equipment

is a black box. Bottle blondes are pilloried for not being natural, for getting their beauty out of a bottle, but such barbs are usually delivered by blonde actresses and models who promote a vast range of shampoos and skincare products . . . many of which come straight out of a bottle.

Life can be great as a bottle blonde. You don't have to travel hundreds of miles to discover your roots. And people are always surprised that you're not as dumb as you look – you don't climb on the roof because you heard drinks were on the house and you don't stare at a carton of orange juice simply because it says 'concentrate'. You even 'get' blonde jokes.

BUDGET AIRLINES

There's nothing wrong with budget airlines. Unless you're the pilot or are a recent winner of a Ronnie Corbett lookalike contest, air travel is always an uncomfortable experience, no matter how much you pay. So why spend more? You may get a nice cushion to put behind your head if you fly with more expensive airlines, but you're still liable to get a truculent child kicking the back of your seat throughout the flight because Mummy won't let him do a wing-walk. Also, with budget airlines you don't have to sit through interminable repeats of *Birds of a Feather* on the in-flight TV, or listen to twenty-five years of Europop on the headphones. Nor do you have to spend ages trying to identify the contents of the in-flight meal; that's before it's sent for forensic analysis and always assuming you've managed to remove the silver-foil lid without suffering third-degree burns. Clue: the answer is usually a cottage pie that looks as if it's recently emerged at speed from a hippo's backside.

Critics complain that some budget airlines land you at an airport in a different hemisphere to your ultimate destination, but travel is surely supposed to be an unpredictable adventure. If it weren't, everyone would just spend their holidays on the Circle Line. And what could be healthier at the start of your holiday than that mad dash across the tarmac to grab a seat which isn't right next to the hen party from Dudley? Furthermore, I have detected that budget airline crews put a little extra verve and add a few new moves to the safety procedure, making it altogether more entertaining, almost along the lines of a Busby Berkeley musical. Watching one flight attendant theatrically indicating the location of the emergency exits, you'd have sworn it was Cyd Charisse.

BUILDERS

Builders are great because any work they do on your house is a bonus. If a TV repairman says he'll come out at 9 a.m., but doesn't show up until midday, you get annoyed. But if a builder does the same, you're delighted that he's bothered to put in an appearance at all. That's because builders work on a different clock to the rest of the population. When they say morning, they mean afternoon (possibly, unless it's raining or there's racing on the telly) and when they say Tuesday, they actually mean

Friday. And because the householder realises this, he or she is never disappointed. It's called customer relations.

There are other reasons why builders are great. As a result of low-slung jeans, there is the phenomenon known as 'builder's bottom', which doesn't occur in any other species and which allows passers-by a glimpse into the darkest recesses of a builder's mind. Builders can also be relied upon to maintain two age-old British traditions – the wolf whistle and the tea break, the latter normally taken, in accordance with regulations laid down by the Federation of Master Builders, within ten minutes of their arrival. In fact if you've got a twenty-gallon vat of tea in the kitchen and don't know what to do with it, just invite a gang of builders.

BUSINESS MEETINGS

The workplace is generally divided up into two types of people: those that do, and those that don't because they are in meetings all day. As the noted economist J. K. Galbraith observed: 'Meetings are indispensable when you don't want to do anything.' Indeed, in certain companies there are people who have spent their entire careers in meetings, and occasionally just the one meeting. By doing so, they are able to avoid anything resembling actual work. And when the meeting finishes, they simply arrange another meeting to discuss the points raised in the first meeting. And so on. The minutes simply fly by, unless there is someone to write them down. While the purpose of endless meetings may be lost on most of us, the benefits to the work-shy and the self-important are immeasurable.

- In meetings, you can listen to the sound of your own voice for hours on end.
- You can make yourself appear a really valuable member of the company.
- While others are talking, you can catch up on your sleep/Sudoku/sexual fantasies.
- You sometimes get cakes.

C

CABBAGE

Show me a boy that enjoyed eating boiled cabbage and I'll show you a freak of nature. But, at least with cabbage on your plate, there was a pretty good chance that there wouldn't be Brussels sprouts too – unless, of course, your mother was a sadist. Also, eating your cabbage – or indeed any greens – earned a child brownie points: perhaps a bag of pear drops to take away the taste, a deferred bedtime, a small step towards getting that elusive Scalextric set or doll's house for Christmas, or being excused having to kiss Great Aunt Hilda and her Zapata moustache. Cabbage was currency.

CALL CENTRES

Trying to negotiate your way through the average call centre is like trying to negotiate Spaghetti Junction on a unicycle. Cobwebs have been known to form on callers before they have finally been put through to an adviser. On the plus side, call-centre instructions teach a higher level of numeracy than most schools. Press 1 if you are calling about your gas bill. Press 2 if you are calling about your gas meter reading. Press 3 if you are calling about your electricity bill. Press 4 if you are calling about your electricity meter reading. Press 5 if you are calling about your gas and electricity bills combined. Press 6 if you would like to have your gas and electricity bills combined. Press 7 if you would like to change your

gas supplier. Press 8 if you would like to win a free trip to Mars. Press 9 if you have been gassed since the start of this call. Call centres also teach you to differentiate between the hash key and the star key on your phone, which must be really important. And call centres are fine provided you use your time on the phone productively. Here are a few things that you can do while waiting to be put through:

- Complete *The Times* crossword.
- Hum Beethoven's Fifth Symphony in its entirety.
- Watch the first series of *Friends* on DVD.
- Correct the mistakes in Einstein's Theory of Relativity.
- Copy the Bayeux Tapestry onto post-it notes.
- Knit a scarf.

CANADIANS

Every country has its favourite whipping boy – another country that is the butt of its jibes and jokes. With England, it is Ireland; with Australia, it is New Zealand; and with the United States, it is the rest of the world. High on the US list is neighbouring Canada, whose inhabitants are generally portrayed by Americans as being staid, ridiculously polite and terminally dull. Yet stars of the calibre of Bryan Adams, Pamela Anderson, Michael J. Fox, Mike Myers, William Shatner, Donald Sutherland and Shania Twain are all Canadian. Equally, Mariah Carey, Tonya Harding, Paris Hilton, O. J. Simpson, Tiffany and Mike Tyson aren't. There are plenty of other good things about being Canadian:

- Canada has the largest French population that never surrendered to Germany.
- Canadians know what to do with all the parts of a buffalo.
- It is so cold in winter, the trunk of a Canadian's car can double as a deep freeze.
- A Canadian political leader can admit to a scandal and see his or her popularity rating rise immediately.
- Driving in Canada is actually safer in winter because the potholes are filled with snow.
- Canadians can meet a moose on Main Street without batting an eyelid.

CANNED LAUGHTER

Often it's the only way you know you're watching a

comedy on TV, so instead of banning canned laughter, there should really be more of it in the world. Let's hear laughter tracks played during weddings, coronations, news bulletins, Budget speeches, courtroom trials, the shipping forecast, and meetings of the United Nations Security Council.

CARAVANS

They may be difficult to overtake but at least towing a caravan prevents drivers doing 80mph down a winding country lane, unless, of course, they deliberately wish to launch the caravan's occupants over a hedge into an adjoining field. Driving a car with a caravan behind is rather like going for a run while towing an adult hippopotamus on roller skates and both activities should be conducted with equal degrees of caution. However, once you have arrived at your destination, caravanning is pure unbridled joy.

Taking a caravan on holiday allows you to be at one with nature, several species of which can often be found in your bed at night. There's no need to worry about booking into a hotel or that the establishment's

facilities don't come up to expectations – in a caravan an alarm call is performed by a Rhode Island Red, the adult movie consists of watching a courting couple scrambling about in the undergrowth, and room service is whatever flies in through the window. As for having a nice deep relaxing bath, it depends how recently the cows' drinking trough was emptied. Above all, caravanning is cheap, cheerful, and you can always return home if a hurricane suddenly develops . . . sometimes quicker than you might anticipate.

JIM CARREY

He's funny, he's hilarious. He pushes back the boundaries of comedy by pulling funny faces.

TOM CAT

In *Tom and Jerry* cartoons, Tom the cat is always seen as the baddie. But this is nothing more than clever spin on behalf of the rodent lobby. In truth, Tom is more victim than villain; a hapless creature forever tormented by a devious mouse. All Tom does is obey his natural instincts to chase mice, but he never really means to harm Jerry in any way that couldn't be cured by a couple of sessions of counselling. Jerry, on the other hand, inflicts all manner of physical pain on poor Tom, from flattening his face with a steam iron to clamping his tail in a vice. And when the going gets tough, he hides behind Spike the bulldog. Yet in the public's eyes, Jerry can do no wrong, simply because he has an angelic face and lives in a hole. So do the Cardiff Male Voice Choir but they don't get any sympathy.

So it is time TV historians reassessed Tom's character in a more favourable light. His only crimes are exuberance and crass stupidity. He's nowhere near as bad as he is painted.

CELEBRITY CHEFS

Rather like magpies, celebrity chefs have tended to multiply in recent years. Ainsley, Gordon, Jamie, Rick, Nick, Nigella, Hugh, Gary, Delia, Wozza – they're everywhere. And these are just the Premiership boys. In the lower leagues there are dozens more, all hoping to rise

like a soufflé and earn their own TV series. But as yet there is no indication that too many cooks spoil the ratings. We love them, despite the fact that Antony Worrall Thompson looks disturbingly like Henry VIII, Delia Smith appears to hit the sauce in a big way when she goes to the football, and Rick Stein has been exposed as a love rat. Yet these are small fry compared to America's own domestic goddess, Martha Stewart, who served five months in jail in 2004 for lying to stock-market regulators. That's as bad as Delia using Pot Noodle in a recipe. Just as Thursday is the new Friday, brown is the new black, and Dick and Dom are the new Trevor and Simon, so cookery is the new gardening . . . which was once the new D-I-Y, which in turn was the new knitting, which was the new lace-making, which was the new penny-farthing riding, which was the new hanging, drawing and quartering.

CELEBRITY STALKERS

You're nobody in Hollywood unless you've had cosmetic surgery, been sued by a member of your own family, or been stalked. Your own stalker is now as much a fashion accessory as a Dolce & Gabbana bag or a pair of Jimmy Choo shoes. Jodie Foster, Catherine Zeta Jones, Gwyneth Paltrow and Halle Berry have all been involved in high-profile cases in which they've been stalked. As a result, they received shedloads of free publicity and public sympathy, and their ordeal probably added a nought to their next movie fee. By contrast, Anna Kournikova had the misfortune to have a hopelessly incompetent stalker.

William Lepeska swam naked across Biscayne Bay to reach the tennis star's Florida home, only to end up at the wrong house, shouting: 'Anna! Save me!' Her embarrassment at Lepeska's ineptness was the talk of the circuit.

There is even a website, Gawker Stalker, where members of the public helpfully report celebrity sightings. '20.49, 3 November 2006, Ethel's Diner, East Street, Portland, William Shatner sitting at table near fire extinguisher, eating double cheeseburger and fries with a medium Diet Coke.' The posting promptly causes a frantic rush to the restaurant so that fans can ambush Shatner before he finishes his apple pie with extra ice cream and a pair of wafers that look like Mr Spock's ears.

But far from being a menace, celebrity stalkers should be encouraged. Although having an ex-stalker is a bit like having your model melted down by Madame Tussaud's to create Claudia Winkleman, it's better than never having even had a stalker. How many C-list celebs would give their right arm to have a stalker? As Shane Richie once remarked: 'The only time I get a stalker is first thing in the morning.' Perhaps universities should run courses for stalkers, so that fully qualified ones can advertise in Yellow Pages between 'stairlifts' and 'stamp dealers'. A stalker makes a celebrity feel wanted. And a stalker isn't just for a day – it's for life. Besides, it's someone to keep you company walking through those dark streets at night.

CELEBRITY WORKOUT DVDS

Every New Year, a gaggle of soap stars and minor celebrities release DVDs instructing us how to shed those extra pounds put on over Christmas. These masterpieces sell in droves, because who wouldn't pay £14.99 to acquire the look of *Coronation Street*'s Janice Battersby? She claims to have shrunk from a size 16 to a size 6, giving us hope that she may soon evaporate altogether. For she still has the sort of face that would look more at home in a tropical fish tank, boasting the ability to strip flesh off a carcass in a matter of seconds.

The real joy is in the rivalry between the celebrities as to whose workout DVD is selling the best. You can envisage the backstage bitching: my lifestyle-altering shape-challenge burns off more calories per minute than yours. It was reported that Michelle McManus's effort was selling slowly at the start of 2007, possibly because someone had made the mistake of putting a picture of her on the cover. Still, you had to admire her guts. And then the papers devote a spread to comparing the DVDs' relative merits and discover – surprise, surprise – that most of them are no more beneficial to our health than walking to the kebab shop.

Workout DVDs featuring young actresses in tight-fitting leotards are ideal for men who can no longer reach up to the top shelf. Also, they often give flagging careers a timely boost and the number of calories used just in trying to get the DVD out of its box and into the player is a positive start towards weight loss. So instead of reducing the number, let's see even more next year. To cater for the older end of the market, what about *Betty Turpin's Walk-In Bath Steps?* And given that Jane Fonda started the craze for celebrity workout videos, you wonder why there haven't been more movie-related fitness DVDs, such as *Pilates of the Caribbean*.

THE CELLO

It's the moment the entire school dreads. At the end-of-term assembly, you've already sat through a precocious pianist and half a dozen unsuccessful attempts to extract a recognisable tune from a recorder when the music teacher announces grandly: 'And now Wilkins of 4C will give a recital on the cello.' Played professionally, the cello sounds variously like long fingernails scraping down a blackboard or a nocturnal fight between two tomcats, but, in the hands of a fourteen-year-old schoolboy, it fails to scale even these heights. How can you tell if a cello is out of tune? – The bow is moving. It is difficult to imagine anyone's life being enriched by the cello. It is music to mourn to. Its permanent air of brooding melancholy could reduce a St Patrick's Day party in Dublin to wholesale depression within a matter of minutes. Yet, scratch beneath the surface – as most cellists seem wont to do – and even the cello has its bright side.

For a start, it has given Julian Lloyd Webber a career, apart from being Andrew's slightly better looking younger brother. In many respects, the cello is an under-used instrument. A strategically positioned cello quartet in a shopping mall would disperse any gang of loitering youths without requiring the intervention of a slow, overweight security guard. Similarly, an endless loop of cello music piped into Taliban caves would flush out Osama bin Laden in no time.

Alternatively, of course, the cello could be used for what was surely God's original intention: firewood.

CHANNEL FIVE

Channel Five gets a lot of stick for broadcasting a steady diet of American imports, football matches that nobody outside Blackburn wants to watch, and for seemingly having an obsession with sex and Hitler. If a programme can somehow combine sex and Hitler, all the better. So titles like *Bonking in the Bunker* or *Hermann Goering and the Art of the Female Orgasm* always stand an excellent chance of being commissioned.

But Channel Five is not all dross. For every Matthew Wright, there is an Austin Stevens, the intrepid South

African wildlife presenter who makes the late Steve Irwin look like David Attenborough. Not to be confused with Steve Austin, the Six Million Dollar Man (although there are definite similarities), Austin Stevens is either utterly fearless or utterly stupid, and possibly both. He never knowingly undersells his programmes. He could turn a Sunday morning spent feeding the ducks in the park into a life-and-death struggle, which would probably culminate in him rolling on the ground with a deadly moorhen. 'These guys can give you a nasty peck if you're not careful! You could lose a limb!'

His speciality is photographing highly venomous snakes, but instead of quietly inviting them along to a studio, he prefers to track them down in the wild, leap on them, wrestle with them and provoke them into aggressive poses that will make for a good photo. Occasionally, the snakes take exception to this treatment and bite him, but fortunately Stevens appears

indestructible. Or at least there is probably the technology to rebuild him.

Every show follows roughly the same format. He treks into the jungle/desert in search of some toxic serpent but can't find a specimen anywhere. He is about to give up when the snake conveniently slithers into view, just after the final commercial break. So our hero gets his pictures and lives to fight another day.

Maybe in his dotage Stevens will calm down with gentler series such as *Austin Stevens: Pet Photographer*. Just don't expect your rabbit to emerge from the session with much fur.

CHEWING GUM

Without chewing gum for ninety minutes (plus extra time), Sir Alex Ferguson would surely have spontaneously combusted years ago. And, whilst gum on city pavements looks unsightly, it does stop frail people getting blown away on a windy day.

CHILDBIRTH

Giving birth has been likened to passing a bowling ball, but it's not all pain and tears. You get bought flowers when he hasn't even done anything wrong and you'll get at least two days off from doing the housework. Well, maybe one if he wants to go out celebrating with his mates.

CHOPSTICKS

There's nothing particularly complicated about using two pieces of wood or plastic to pick up food. I have yet to encounter a pair of chopsticks that come with a full operating manual. Yet people always seem disproportionately impressed if you can use them. 'Ooh, aren't you clever?' they trill, as if you've just split the atom or discovered the North-West Passage. So, while they are implements ill designed for the job (you wouldn't by choice eat roast beef and Yorkshire pudding with a pair of knitting needles), chopsticks are really useful for making you look good. And anything that can do that is always welcome.

CHRISTMAS CRACKER JOKES

They may be corny, but at least nobody will die laughing at them. That's a good thing, because a sudden death at the table tends to spoil Christmas dinner. And the gravy goes cold while you're trying to reach over the corpse for the stuffing.

COFFEE CREAMS

Rather like the class fattie at football, the coffee cream is nearly always the last to be picked. What have others in the box of chocolates got that it hasn't? Hard caramels are really boring and normally take out half your teeth, soft caramels are sickly and stick to your gums for days, and Belgian chocolates are simply more chocolate inside a chocolate, which seems distinctly unimaginative. Then there are half a dozen containing different types of nut, invariably surrounded by caramel or Belgian chocolate, and a wafer that is a pale imitation of a Kit-Kat, so that the only ones that truly stand out are the orange and coffee creams. And the orange creams always go first because that seems to be the first rule of chocoholics. Meanwhile, the poor old coffee cream is left to gather dust after all the other centres have been devoured. Sometimes it is even held over and added to the next box in the hope that a visitor may declare a secret fondness. So it's about time someone spoke up for the coffee cream. Justice for the coffee cream! Free the Black Magic two!

COLD CALLERS

Cold callers are not to be confused with nuisance callers. Although cold callers are a nuisance. And they do make calls. So is that clear? Cold callers fall into two categories – the ones who ring you up out of the blue when you're halfway through dinner, trying to sell you a new kitchen, and the ones who knock at your door, offering to tarmac your drive for £5 (plus any unforeseen extras, which usually total around £5,000). Yet cold callers can be welcome in some households. For the lonely, the shy or the downright unpopular, an unexpected visitor or caller can be the highlight of the week. And when the calls are silent, having been selected at random by computer, it can be like receiving a dirty phone call, which might inject new life into barren relationships. Plenty of women have given up hope of ever hearing heavy breathing again. Getting rid of unwanted callers at the door is also excellent practice for dealing with an emergency situation at speed. In the event of a fire, you might only have a split second to tell your family, 'QUICK! OUT OF THE HOUSE! FRONT DOOR!' So to a cold caller, see how quickly you can say, 'NO! NOT INTERESTED! BUGGER OFF!'

COMPETITIVE DADS

Whether it's Scrabble, tennis or who can peel a banana the fastest, there are some fathers who have to beat their sons at everything. And what's wrong with that, provided you don't cheat or go to the extremes of giving high-fives to passers-by after defeating a three-year-old at crazy golf or chant 'you're not winning anymore' after discovering who really did have Mr Bun the Baker? Boys are naturally competitive. It's in their make-up, although it's sometimes less marked in those who actually wear make-up. Letting them win at everything will simply give them a false impression of their own ability. I bet Tim Henman's dad always let him win, whereas Roger Federer's was probably a mean bastard.

As long as it's not too demoralising, a spot of healthy competition is good for building up character. After all, being competitive is often all that separates men from plant life. So pay no attention to those bleeding hearts who have abolished school sports in favour of group therapy or who want to make the whole class equal winners, competition is here to stay. If there were no competitive sports or competitive dads, where would England have found its Ashes heroes? OK, so that's probably not a good example.

CONFESSIONAL TV

Jerry Springer, Oprah, Trisha, The Jeremy Kyle Show; don't you just love them? It's always so reassuring to watch these shows and realise that other people's lives are infinitely worse than your own. Somehow a stolen kiss with a married colleague at the office party pales in comparison to the woman who is having regular sex with a zebra. And why do they go on national television to be roundly condemned by the baying audience and the judgmental presenter? And the zebra took a fair bit of stick, too.

The fact is that, with most of us leading relatively humdrum lives, confessional TV offers a form of escapism, rather like jockeys watching *The World's Strongest Man*, nuns tuning in to *The Perfect Penis*, or comedians watching *My Family*. To make sure that the genre continues for many years to come, here are a few suggestions for future topics:

- I'm Caught In A Love Hexagon.
- How Can I Cure My Teacosy Fetish?
- My Psychiatrist Doesn't Understand Me.
- I'm In Love With My Best Friend's Gerbil.
- The Woman Who Thinks She Is My Daughter Is Really My Niece, The Man Who Thinks He Is My Younger Brother Is Really My Son, And The Boy Who Thinks I'm His Grandpa Doesn't Know That I'm Really His Grandma.
- I'm Having An Affair With A Wedding Cake Decorator – Will It End In Tiers?

CONSPIRACY THEORIES

The world is full of conspiracy theories. Did Apollo 11 really touch down on the Moon? Was JFK killed on orders from the CIA? Did an alien spacecraft land at Roswell in 1947? Has there been a government cover-up to hide the truth behind 9/11? Is Elvis alive and well and working in the Memphis branch of Burger King? And was Princess Diana murdered, perhaps at the request of the British royal family? These theories are all probably nonsense but they keep cynics in business and provide hours of entertaining reading on the Internet. So until the next big one comes along, here are a few new conspiracy theories that deserve investigation:

● Was Shergar really two Dartmoor ponies stitched together?
● Was Florence Nightingale Jack the Ripper?
● Is there a dodo that is still alive and living at a secret address on the Costa del Sol?
● Was Bernard Manning Prince Andrew's real father?
● Was Humpty Dumpty pushed?
● Is George W. Bush really just a cardboard cut-out?
● Are Bob Hoskins and Danny DeVito the same person?
● Did Donald Duck send out coded messages to the KGB?

COUCH POTATOES

The trouble with modern life is that so many people run around like headless chickens, forever chasing their tail . . . except that without a head they'd have nothing with which to chase it and with no eyes (because they've got no head) they wouldn't even be able to see where their tail was, let alone chase it. But you get my drift. Couch potatoes

don't suffer from this affliction. They don't live life in the fast lane, they live it in the bus lane.

Medical experts say it's unhealthy to be a couch potato, omitting to point out, however, that the lack of exercise is comfortably offset by the sort of low stress levels usually associated with someone who is either immensely content with every aspect of life or is in a coma. When was the last time you heard of a couch potato suffering a fatal heart attack, and if they did, how could anyone tell? The first sign would be an unpleasant decaying smell coming from the sofa area, followed several weeks later by a gradual loosening of the grip on the TV remote control.

A couch potato is such an undemanding soul, so easy to please. He (and they are usually men) doesn't need fast cars, new clothes or even clean underwear, all he requires for a blissful existence is custody of the remote. He's not even bothered about having something decent to watch – he'll sit there glued to any programme. *Bob the Builder* or *Newsnight*, it's all the same to a couch potato. The only things calculated to disrupt a couch potato's customary cool are the batteries running out in the aforementioned remote, the public stoning of David Dickinson, total transmitter failure, or the sofa catching fire . . . although naturally he would wait until the next commercial break before calling the emergency services.

SIMON COWELL

Simon Cowell has done more to give hope to the underprivileged of the world than anyone since Mother Teresa. Simon allows our dreams – no matter how far-fetched – to become reality. Because if Gareth Gates, Michelle McManus and Steve Brookstein can become famous for longer than a nanosecond, there is hope for everyone.

CROCODILES

There are many adjectives that can be applied to crocodiles, but 'cuddly' isn't one of them. Even inflatable crocodiles look vaguely menacing as they glide across the hotel pool. Any minute you think they're going to rise out of the water, snatch a German holidaymaker off his sunbed and perform a death roll in the shallow end. Tales of reptilian ferocity are legendary. After a killer croc had grabbed his friend, a guy in Australia was forced to spend the entire night clinging precariously to a small tree while the beast returned and circled him in the water below. All he could see were the croc's evil eyes glistening in the dark. Hundreds of people are killed by crocodiles every year, usually unfortunates who for some reason decide to cool off near that giant log floating in the water. Even supposedly less aggressive alligators were responsible for three fatal attacks in Florida in the space of just two weeks in 2006. These creatures are no respecters of the tourist industry.

But aren't crocodiles simply taking revenge for all the handbags and pairs of shoes that they have unwillingly provided? And by snatching the foolish and the unwary, it could be argued that they are merely thinning the herd. In view of the number of crocodile attacks in Australia, surely we should be encouraging them to infiltrate the *I'm a Celebrity* . . . jungle set in Queensland. What a service they could have done to mankind in 2006, although Jan Leeming would probably have been too much for even a crocodile to stomach. The late Steve Irwin owed his entire career to crocodiles, who probably wept human tears on hearing of his death. Equally Captain Hook would never have become a memorable pantomime character had not a crocodile bitten off his hand.

Despite their bad reputation, crocodiles are surprisingly gentle and caring parents, tenderly cradling the babies in their powerful jaws. No social worker has ever taken a baby croc into care. There is even the possibility that, in future, crocodiles may be of medicinal value as scientists in the United States believe that a dose of crocodile blood could help conquer certain human infections that are immune to standard antibiotics. Mind you, it might put off a few regular blood donors to arrive at the clinic and find a 20 foot-long crocodile waiting to give blood.

Instead of dwelling on the negatives, let's focus on some of the things that crocodiles can't be blamed for during their

200 million years on the planet. No crocodile has ever released a Christmas novelty single. No crocodile has ever worn socks with sandals. No crocodile has ever tried to defraud the taxman, although they've probably eaten a few. No crocodile has ever married for money. No crocodile has ever read a Jeffrey Archer novel. No crocodile has ever worn a toupee. No crocodile has ever voted Republican.

CYCLISTS

Cyclists have long had a bad press, but who has been responsible for the negativity? Motorists: those gas-guzzling pollutants who pound the streets running over the elderly, the slow and the drunk. Yet motorists reckon that cyclists are a menace on the road – in the same way they believe that other motorists, white lines and speed restrictions are also a menace on the road. So it's time someone spoke up for cyclists: a bicycle spokesman. Cyclists are great. They are environmentally friendly, generally polite, they wash their hands before dinner, they are kind to their mothers and they constitute the world's major market for the sale of cycle clips.

D

DARTS

Some scribes have had the effrontery to suggest that darts is not a proper sport, simply because the distance walked from oche to board takes less time and effort than to circumnavigate Andy Fordham. How can anyone say that the likes of Leighton Rees, Jocky Wilson and Bobby George were not true athletes? You only have to look at them. George must be fit just to be able to carry that amount of jewellery.

Darts combines two of men's favourite pastimes – drinking and throwing things – and over the years it has been a godsend for manufacturers of extra-extra-large shirts. Also, without darts there would be no Sid Waddell – the TV commentator whose classic descriptions of these gladiatorial contests include 'His eyes are bulging like the belly of a hungry chaffinch', 'That was like throwing three pickled onions into a thimble', and 'These guys look calm but inside they are as nervous as a vampire who knows there's a sale at the wooden-stake shop in the morning.' You don't get that from John Motson.

DENTISTS

They charge an exorbitant amount of money for inflicting grievous pain when you could do it yourself for the price of a hammer. But they will point out that it's worth paying what is almost tantamount to a second mortgage just to ensure that you have a dentist without blood on his gown or one whose idea of a modern dental practice is a length of string and a doorknob. And when you think about it, a visit to the dentist isn't all bad.

- You get to taste exciting new flavours of mouthwash.
- You learn lots of new things about your gums, like how readily they bleed when a sharp hook is jabbed into them.
- You'll never have a better chance of studying a ceiling.
- You can get a really good close-up of a drill bit.
- You find teeth you never knew you had.
- You can practise opening your mouth really wide – invaluable if you ever intend swallowing a whole roast chicken.
- You can listen to the soothing sounds of Classic FM, although the music is sometimes drowned out by screams from the adjoining room.
- You can find out where your dentist has been on his six holidays this year with the money he's made from your fees.

DIARRHOEA

It may be embarrassing and uncomfortable, but you'll never really know how fast you can run until you've got diarrhoea.

DIRE STRAITS

History tells us that, with the exception of her marriage, everything Princess Diana touched turned to gold. Well, that wasn't the case with Dire Straits. No sooner had she confessed that they were one of her favourite bands than their street cred plummeted and they acquired an undeserved reputation for blandness. They were granted full membership of the easy-listening circle, doomed to be played by Jimmy Young on Radio 2. You could have understood the reaction if the fan had been Prince Charles, a man who danced the Twist in a manner that suggested he'd just come round from a heavy anaesthetic. And anyway who were these people that poured scorn on Mark Knopfler and co.? Mostly they were disciples of bands like The Smiths. Morrissey would never be tainted by royal patronage, they droned. Morrissey's a real poet. Morrissey's got principles. Yeah, and in 2007 Morrissey was offering to represent the UK in the Eurovision Song Contest . . .

Dire Straits play James Last

DISCOUNT SOFA SALES

Every day, somewhere in the UK, a discount sofa sale is either starting or ending. Except they never end, do they? After it has been announced 'Sale Must End Sunday', we learn that the sale has been extended for another week. And so on it goes. And on. And on. It is rumoured that a DFS sale in Droitwich has been running since 1987. Whereas once Britain was a nation of shopkeepers, it now seems that we're a nation of sofa manufacturers.

All of this means it has never been easier – or cheaper – to buy a sofa. We may face water shortages and food rationing as a result of climate change but we'll always be able to buy a brown-leather corner unit.

DOG BREATH

Dog breath may be revolting but without it incidents of bestiality would probably go through the roof.

DUST

House dust appears to serve little purpose beyond looking unsightly and making you sneeze, but without dust you wouldn't know where you had missed while cleaning the room. And don't forget, dust is largely composed of old skin. Isn't it better that your discarded skin forms a layer on a table top rather than just hanging in shreds off your body so that you look like a lizard that has been through a cheese grater?

E

EARWAX

When God designed the human ear, why did he get it to produce wax? Bees have pretty much got mass wax production sewn up, so why couldn't He have made the human ear produce something useful like chocolate? Or oil? That way Dubya wouldn't have needed to stick his stupid nose in the Middle East. He wouldn't have known Iraq from Tie Rack, although there is still a suspicion that he gets the two confused as was shown recently when the manager of the Euston Station branch was surprised to find 500 US Marines reporting for duty. Luckily it was the first day of the sale.

Quite apart from the fact that it will make you deaf if you leave it to fester, earwax doesn't appear to offer a great deal in terms of life enhancement. But if you collect enough of it in a jar over a period of years, you will eventually be able to polish your car for free. The other great thing about earwax is that once you've accidentally tasted the stuff, you'll never do it again.

ESTATE AGENTS

If he'd been around today, Uriah Heep would surely have been an estate agent, where he could be 'ever so 'umble' while fleecing homeowners of their hard-earned cash for doing sod all. Estate agents are seemingly trained to be cloying and obsequious. They're about as genuine as *The Hitler Diaries* and not nearly as interesting. They are like windscreen wipers – wet, flaccid, moving from side to side, and bowing and scraping when you look at them. They're oilier than a very oily oil slick.

You wouldn't mind if they actually did anything. How can taking a photo of a house, putting an ad in a newspaper and conducting a few guided tours warrant charging £4,500 on a £300,000 house? And when they turn up at your house for their initial sales pitch, they stay for hours. Dry rot is easier to get rid of.

So what redeeming features do estate agents possess? Well, because they are so unbearably self-absorbed, they rarely breed outside their species, if at all. Also, the introduction of estate agents has enabled axe murderers and the common garden slug to move a rung up the evolutionary ladder. Estate agents make you realise that a personalised pen is no substitute for a personality, and, in times of crisis, they make great human body shields.

Furthermore, regardless of whether you're selling or buying, estate agents are paid to be nice to you at all times.

PROSPECTIVE BUYER: You're a complete tosser, aren't you?

ESTATE AGENT: Quite probably, sir. Let me show you the unique features in the kitchen . . .

PROSPECTIVE BUYER: No, I mean it. You really are a Grade A arsehole, a man of hidden shallows. You are living proof that manure can grow legs and walk.

ESTATE AGENT: Ceramic hob, with built-in oak-effect cupboards above . . .

PROSPECTIVE BUYER: When they made you, they broke the mould but some of it grew back.

ESTATE AGENT: Absolutely, sir. Plumbing for a dish-washer . . .

PROSPECTIVE BUYER: You're so two-faced, I bet you don't know which one to wash in the morning. In fact I despise you so much, I'm going to cut your tie with these scissors. There!

ESTATE AGENT: Very nice, sir. And there's a newly installed waste disposable unit in the sink . . .

PROSPECTIVE BUYER: And I'm going to squeeze ketchup all over your suit. Like this.

ESTATE AGENT: Don't worry, sir. It's due to be cleaned

anyway. All the windows are fully double glazed with a fifteen-year guarantee . . .

PROSPECTIVE BUYER: And I'm going to cut off your ear with this pizza slicer.

ESTATE AGENT: Ah. Never mind, it only hurts a bit, and I've always been a fan of mono sound. Have I told you about the deceptively spacious utility room with possible use as a granny flat?

EUROVISION SONG CONTEST

The Eurovision Song Contest is an annual treat, along with Wimbledon, the Oscars, and Michael Owen's comeback from injury. It brings you the joys of Terry Wogan's wry commentary, the anticipation of seeing who will finish on nul points, and the wonderful political voting. Greece never fails to award Cyprus twelve points and vice-versa, all the Baltic and Balkan countries vote for each other, but nobody votes for the United Kingdom, partly because of the war in Iraq, partly because nobody likes us anyway, and partly because our songs are always crap.

Over the past half century Eurovision has brought us such unforgettable titles as 'Pump Pump' (Finland, 1976), 'Boum Badaboum' (Monaco, 1967), 'Bana Bana' (Turkey, 1989), 'A-Ba-Ni-Bi' (Israel, 1978) and Lulu's immortal 'Boom Bang-a-Bang' (UK, 1969). Spain's winning 1968 entry, 'La La La', contained no fewer than 138 la's, thus crossing the language divide at a stroke. Genius! Never let it be said, however, that all Eurovision songs are banal.

Norway's 1960 entry, 'Voi-Voi', was an arrangement of a Lapp reindeer-herding call and their 1980 song was about the construction of a hydro-electric power station – a subject all too often overlooked by popular music lyricists. Sadly the song's message appeared lost on most of the voters, as it came only sixteenth out of nineteen.

Eurovision is invariably good for a spot of controversy and bitchiness, such as when transsexual Dana International (the 'woman' with a name like an airport and a face like a 747) won for Israel in 1998, or when BBC presenter Ray Moore caused a diplomatic incident after jokingly referring to the Turkish group as 'an ugly crowd'. When a thirteen-year-old schoolgirl, Sandra Kim, steered Belgium to victory in 1986, France and Israel were quick to jump on the bandwagon, fielding an eleven-year-old girl and a twelve-year-old boy respectively in 1989. There was widespread condemnation following the UK announcement that it was entering a foetus for the 1990 Eurovision.

As for the quality of the performers, don't forget Celine Dion represented Switzerland in the 1988 contest, a reminder that standards are always likely to slip occasionally.

Above all, the Eurovision offers the little countries the chance to shine. Latvia, Monaco, Estonia, Luxembourg, Switzerland – they may never win the World Cup or invade anybody, but they've triumphed at the Eurovision Song Contest. What greater glory could there be?

EXPENSIVE COCKTAILS

A dash of vermouth, a splash of gin, half a carton of orange juice and a sparkler? That'll be £8.50. Still, when you've spent that much money on one drink, at least there's none left for you to end up in the gutter at the end of the evening.

FACIAL PIERCING

Nose studs, lip rings, tongue studs, eyebrow rings. Some people have so many metal facial piercings that the only thing attracted to them is a magnet. Although the fashion statement might not be to everyone's taste, there are one or two beneficial side effects from covering your face in metal adornments:

- You can get Radio 5 anywhere in the country.

- Wearing a lip stud to school will earn you more time off than any sick note from your mum.
- They're a conversation piece, especially when they go septic.
- After a car crash, you couldn't possibly look any worse than you did before.

FAKE TANS

The orange look is vastly underrated. You could become the face of a multi-national mobile phone corporation, you could be mistaken for a Dutch football fan (which at least gives you a chance of supporting a successful team), or you could get modelling work as a satsuma. So you see, there's nothing wrong with being orange. The future's bright . . .

FAST FOOD

In the United States alone, consumers spend $140 billion a year on fast food. This statistic could be interpreted variously as indicating that a) Americans have no taste, b) there are a lot of fast food outlets in the US or c) fast food is actually rather good.

Fast food has changed our lives – and generally for the better. Obviously if you eat burgers or pizza every day for every meal it's not very healthy, but as long as you intersperse fast food with plenty of proper food, there's no real problem. Like visiting relatives or reading James Joyce, fast food should be taken in moderation. Even then, it can be a challenge to identify precisely which part of the chicken you are eating at a fast food chicken restaurant. Fast food restaurants have come in for some criticism over their pay and conditions but really they should be applauded for giving jobs to people who would otherwise be unemployable. They are also equal opportunity employers, never put off by such conditions as rampant acne. Anyway a pus-filled face is always handy in case they run short of relish.

THE FLYING NUN

This sixties American sitcom about the adventures of Sister Bertrille may have lacked the wit of, say, *M*A*S*H* or *The Money Programme*, but it did give actress Sally Field her big break. And in a world where so many TV shows are derivative, this has been the only one about a nun who flies. So far.

THE GEORGE FOREMAN GRILL

If a former world heavyweight boxing champion says his lean, mean grilling machine is great, only a brave man or an idiot would argue with him.

FOUR-WHEEL DRIVES

It has been argued that nobody should be allowed to drive a 4x4 unless they are actually on safari. Doing the school run is apparently not an excuse, because how many rampaging rhino and charging buffalo are you likely to encounter on a Wednesday morning in Thames Ditton? Have these whingers never heard of safari parks? You never know when a lion is likely to escape from Woburn or Longleat, and when one does, you want to be sitting in a Mitsubishi Shogun, not a Smart car. Being at the wheel of a four-wheel drive also lets you go almost eyeball to eyeball with lorry drivers, instead of them towering over you like Arnold Schwarzenegger about to swat a fly. Also, 4x4s are so high off the ground that you never know when you've accidentally run somebody over. So you don't have to listen to the children in the back screaming, 'Mum! You've run over the school-crossing patrol lady!' The first the little darlings know about it will be when the head teacher makes a sad announcement at assembly.

G

GERMANS

What have the Germans ever done to us . . . apart from trying to extend their borders in much the same way as the British have done throughout history? Yet more than sixty years on from the last scuffle, there are sections of

the British public who still claim to hate the Germans, although significantly this attitude is largely prevalent among those whose experience of combat is limited to a drunken brawl outside the local KFC on a Saturday night. We claim that the Germans have no sense of humour – this from a nation that has brought the world Cannon and Ball, Jeremy Beadle and *The Vicar of Dibley*. We moan that the Germans always get up at the crack of dawn to claim the sunbeds on holiday, but that only happens because the British are invariably too hungover to reach the pool much before 11 a.m. We gripe that the Germans always beat us at sport – but virtually every nation in the world beats us at sport. We mock German efficiency, but what wouldn't we give for an efficient rail network, postal service etc.? Contrary to popular belief, most Germans are kind and courteous. The only crime for which they can currently be held responsible is that of trying to force an inferior variety of sausage onto us.

GLOBAL WARMING

'Global warming. Is it really a bad thing? Over to our reporter at the Copacabana Beach, Aberdeen.'

GNOMES (GARDEN)

They may not be to everyone's liking but they're cheery little fellows and, unlike most other things in the garden, they don't need feeding, watering or pruning, unless you're planning on giving your gnome a vasectomy. Unlike birds they don't pull up your newly planted seeds, unlike cats they don't crap all over the garden, and unlike you they don't keel over from having rosy red cheeks.

GOLDFISH

Goldfish have come under fire for having the intelligence and attention span of Jade Goody. Why single out goldfish? When was the last time you saw a halibut on *Mastermind* or a trout on *The Weakest Link* (apart from Anne Robinson, that is)? Fish as a species can't be that bright or they wouldn't keep getting caught. We are told that eating fish makes you more intelligent but it's difficult to see how. It's certainly never worked for the fish. Even so, goldfish are among the most inoffensive creatures on earth. They are harmless and undemanding, they swim around the same stretch of water for years on end without looking bored, and they have the sense not to taste good with vinegar and chips. They also have their own credit card. And when it comes to endangered species and reduced fishing quotas, it's not the goldfish that is likely to be extinct by 2046. So, Mr Cod, who's clever now?

GOLF FANS

Apart from dressing in clothes which give the distinct impression that they are being worn for a bet, and insisting on playing in all weathers and sometimes in light that requires the presence of a torch to find the ball, golfers are a moderately sensible breed. Until, that is, they become fans at major tournaments. Then all intelligence and decorum seem to fly out the window as they revel in yelling inanities such as 'In the hole!' the moment the ball has left the club-head. Or scream 'You the man!' to every golfer even if the player's score currently stands at 28 over par and they've just six-putted.

Yet without these fairway fanatics, watching golf on television would be a bit like, well, watching grass grow. They inject much-needed life and passion into a sport that, even at its most exciting, rarely moves at a pace faster than sedentary. Their unbridled enthusiasm puts to shame followers of other games for whom encouragement is restricted to a ripple of applause. How much more exhilarating chess would be if punctuated by spectator cries of 'Get the bishop!' or 'Mate! Mate! Mate!'

GOTHS

Being a Goth must be great because you never have to think about what colour clothes to wear each day. Also, you don't have to be a slave to fashion although you know you'll always be fashionable one day every year – Halloween.

GRAFFITI

One day graffiti will be recognised as a significant art form rather than mindless vandalism. I can see it happening. The writing's on the wall.

HALF-FULL CRISP PACKETS

Have you noticed how a lot of potato crisp packets are no longer transparent so that you can't see how full the bag is? And when you open it, you find it's half empty. There aren't even any green ones: the rest is just air. Yet really the crisp manufacturers are doing us a favour, because a half-full crisp packet is considerably less fattening than a full one. So instead of complaining about their underhand tactics, we should be grateful to them for prolonging our lives. Let's campaign for packets of chocolate biscuits that consist of one biscuit and a wad of padding or family-sized ice cream tubs containing just one scoop. Anyway, Walkers say that air gives their crisps 'a first day fresh taste. Air helps protect crisps and prevents breakage. Tests have proved that it is important for our consumers to buy packs with as many whole crisps as possible. To achieve this, we must have sufficient air fill and a well-sealed pack.' So there.

HEAD LICE

They can earn you a few days off school in the case of a really bad infestation. Besides, it's nice to give a home to a living creature.

HEALTH AND SAFETY

Health-and-safety regulations have unquestionably made the world a better place. Christmas lights, hanging baskets and CCTV cameras have all been banned or removed from their positions by local councils in Britain because of the very real dangers they might pose to the public in the event of a sudden earthquake measuring above 7.9 on the Richter Scale. The fact that no such event has occurred in the Home Counties over the past 3,000 years is no reason for complacency. A pantomime in Preston was forced to consider scrapping the tradition of the cast throwing sweets into the audience in case someone was injured by a flying sherbet lemon. Meanwhile in Beverley, East Yorkshire, officials decreed that reindeer posed a hygiene risk to the thousands of people who turned out for the annual festive parade. It was ruled that anyone who touched the animals should be made to wash their hands immediately, and, to this end, an official walked alongside the reindeer at the parade, carrying antiseptic wipes.

All very sensible, because the reindeer have almost certainly been pulling a sleigh through skies contaminated by high levels of pollution. Yet what thanks do the unsung individuals who enforce these regulations so rigorously receive for protecting the public? None whatsoever. Instead they are accused of being killjoys and of fostering a 'nanny state'. On the contrary, the only problem with health and safety is that the regulations don't go far enough.

Take trees for example. In strong winds, they are

always blowing down onto houses and cars. They are clearly a hazard and should either all be dug up (and this applies to the Amazon rainforest, too) or lopped to a height not exceeding 1.25 metres.

Airplanes. Each year more people are killed by plane crashes than by falling meteorites. And it's not just the passengers. You never know when a plane is suddenly going to fall out of the sky and land on you. Such an accident could result in your being off work for several weeks, leading to possible compensation claims by your employer. Therefore air travel must be scrapped.

More accidents happen in the home than anywhere else, and it's not difficult to see why. The dinner table alone is an accident simply waiting to happen. Metal knives and forks could take out somebody's eye if used incorrectly. The blade and prongs should either be fitted at all times with small rubber caps to reduce the risk or households should be forced to use only white plastic knives and forks. Condiments should be banned. A small child playfully throwing pepper could cause blindness while the practice of tossing a handful of salt over one's shoulder to bring good luck could have precisely the opposite effect. The sudden movement and contortion of the body could easily result in shoulder dislocation.

Much has been done to reduce the risk of injury in the workplace, but dangerous implements such as paper clips, rubber bands and drawing pins can still be found on many desks. Do you realise the damage that could be done if someone came at you with an unfurled paper clip?

Clothing is another area of concern. The problems

posed by high heels are well documented. In Essex there were 129 recorded cases of heel-related injuries on one windy Saturday night in 2006. This is obviously not acceptable. Therefore flat shoes should be made compulsory in all walks of life, although exceptional cases (such as Tom Cruise) may apply for special dispensation.

Finally, sport. Injuries are all too common on the fields of recreation, so it is time we looked at the health-and-safety aspect. In future, the Ashes should be played with plastic bats and tennis balls. Although eager to preserve the competitive nature of football as a contact sport, players should be made to wear flip flops instead of boots

to reduce injury in the tackle, or indeed any other area of the body. Furthermore, in acknowledgement of the dangers of referees accidentally swallowing their whistles, they should in future carry in their breast pocket a pre-recorded tape of a whistling sound, which can be activated when required. And all matches should be attended by no more than fifty spectators and 600 police officers to ensure crowd safety. Elsewhere, golf should be played with ping-pong balls, all darts should be made of rubber, and Olympic swimmers should wear water wings in case they suddenly forget how to swim. Motor racing speeds should be restricted to 30mph, horse racing should consist of jockeys riding on a fairground carousel, and boxing should be banned altogether, to be replaced by a good argument.

So let's not hear any more complaints about health and safety. You know it makes sense.

HEAT MAGAZINE

Ewan McGregor has called for a boycott of *heat* magazine, labelling it a 'dirty, filthy piece of shit', inserting the adjectives presumably to distinguish it from any other piece of shit. His objection is apparently the magazine's use of paparazzi photos that sometimes show celebrities in an unflattering light, such as Chris Moyles without a paper bag over his head. But it's an accepted fact that publicity is a minor celebrity's oxygen, and celebrities don't come any more minor than those featured in *heat*. *Big Brother* contestants, UKTV Style presenters and

members of Girls Aloud would rather be featured wearing a dodgy frock than not be seen at all. Because it's rather like a professional footballer being kicked out by Forest Green Rovers; if you consider yourself a celebrity and can't get into *heat*, there's nowhere lower to go. You might as well give up. Anyway heat has enough knockers without Ewan McGregor adding to the list. With a circulation of over half a million, it must be doing something right. It's bright, it's brash, and it tells readers how they, too, can look like Jade Goody . . . unless they have corrective surgery. You can buy Jessica Simpson's wardrobe for £80 (£120 if she throws in the dressing table), learn about Dean Gaffney's favourite disease, Pete Burns's make-up secrets, read the truth about Paris Hilton and the Bishop of Southwark (are they more than just friends?), and read how Abi Titmuss has recently been seen in a supermarket, buying, wait for it, food! And *heat* is the perfect place to catch a glimpse of Catherine Zeta Jones or see a snatch of Lindsay Lohan. *Heat* may be vacuous but if you're stuck in a doctor's waiting room for three-quarters of an hour, surrounded by old dears with hacking coughs and a wealth of stories about varicose veins, flicking through its pages is a more entertaining way of passing the time than reading the January 1992 edition of *Horse & Hound*.

HELL

Why should you fear going to Hell when you die? It might be better than you think. In Hell, you'd never need to have the central heating on, you'd never have to listen to a Daniel O'Donnell album, and you'd never have any problems finding a lawyer.

HICCUPS

In 1922, Charles Osborne of Anthon, Iowa, developed hiccups while trying to weigh a hog before slaughter. The hiccups continued unabated for another sixty-eight years, finally stopping in 1990. Alas, Osborne had little time to enjoy the release from his torment, because he died a year later. In his lifetime he is believed to have hiccupped 430 million times, but it is doubtful whether he actually counted them. If he had, he might have found a cure, especially if he had done it while holding his breath, although, alternatively, this could have caused him to die considerably earlier.

At first glance, there's nothing good you can say about hiccups. They always occur at the most inopportune moments – during sex, during your marriage ceremony just after the vicar asks if there are any objections, during sex, during a sponsored vow of silence, during sex, while reading the Ten O'Clock News, during sex, during your driving test, or during sex. However there are occasions when a bout of hiccups could prove useful. If you are trapped beneath the rubble of a collapsed building, hiccups could help the emergency services locate you. Hiccups are also advantageous should you wish to become better acquainted with a Spanish Bull Frog, since they perfectly mimic the sound of its mating call. Hiccups are good if you like being slapped on the back or if you're worried that nobody is paying you any attention. Hiccups are good in a blazing row, because you always have the last word, that word being 'hic'. Hiccups give you something on which to focus – when you've got hiccups, you forget about all your other troubles. So basically hiccups are cool, although it's probably best if they don't last for sixty-eight years.

HOLIDAYS IN BRITAIN

Holidaying in Britain has been desperately unfashionable even longer than kipper ties. But although there's a risk that your hotelier may be a Nora Batty clone with a list of regulations to rival the Maastricht Treaty, that you may be locked out for the night if you arrive back after 10 p.m., that you may lose a limb trying to put up a reluctant deckchair or, most alarming of all, Jim Davidson may be appearing near you in summer season, there's still plenty to recommend a British seaside holiday.

- The weather is never a disappointment because you know in advance that you're going to get at least two wet days a week, one almost certainly being on a

Sunday when everywhere indoors is closed.

- You're unlikely to get travel sick, unless crossing the Devon border brings you out in a rash.
- You won't miss any episodes of *Emmerdale*.
- You don't have to listen to any holiday reps.
- You don't have to mug up on another language, although it might prove advisable if holidaying within the Scouse catchment area (i.e. Southport to Rhyl).
- There's no longer any danger of being invaded by the Radio 1 Roadshow.
- You get proper fish and chips – not an endless supply of hake or every other Mediterranean fish that tastes just like hake.
- Your postcards arrive home before you do.
- You're never far from a model village.

HOODIES

The fashion for teenage boys to skulk around with their hoods up has been declared a cause for grave concern. Some shopping malls have even banned hoodies in case they scare their security guards. But hoodies do serve a purpose – they are aesthetically pleasing in that without them, we would be able to see teenage boys' faces, complete with their pierced eyebrows, nose studs, and sculpted hair with PISS OFF engraved into the scalp. Indeed, far from hoodies being a curse of modern society, it could be argued that they don't go far enough in hiding faces and that all boys should be issued with compulsory balaclavas from the age of twelve. Besides, of all the really nasty people in history – Hitler, Mussolini, Fanny Cradock – how many wore hoods? Is there any footage of Hitler at the Nuremberg Rally in a Nike hooded top? I don't think so. Unless you count Simon Cowl, the only notorious individual to have been associated with a hood was Robin Hood, and he never really hurt anyone – well, apart from the Sheriff of Nottingham's men and they were so dim they had it coming. It's never clever to stand under trees when you know that's where the enemy is hiding.

HUGH GRANT

He may have the range of a paper aeroplane, but he is a genuine British star in Hollywood – and those are about as plentiful as tax rebates. The Divine Brown episode would have wrecked most careers but Grant's public apology and apparent humility actually won him new admirers. Here was someone who could handle a scandal without the help of Max Clifford. Plus he has been rude with Liz Hurley – lots of times. And one of his middle names is Mungo.

I

ICE SKATING

Ice skating is great because it offers so much potential for disaster. Imagine if Torvill and Dean had fallen through the ice, or if some Canadian girl had landed safely from a triple salchow only to break an ankle tripping over the bouquet of flowers that had been thrown onto the rink, or if a lost polar bear suddenly sauntered onto the ice and ate the Russian champion halfway through her compulsory programme. Sadly none of these things ever seem to happen.

IKEA

A trip to IKEA is like visiting a flat-pack fairyland. Everywhere you look there are enchanting sights – draw dividers, CD racks, pine coffee tables, fondue sets, plant stands, dog beds, faucets, pot holders, aprons. If you urgently need a draw divider, maybe as a present for that special someone or for a forthcoming dinner party, isn't it reassuring to know exactly where you can buy one? In fact there are 5,000 products in the IKEA catalogue, which has become something of a shopper's bible. Around 180 million copies are printed each year – triple that of the less consumer-oriented Bible. Such is the clamour for IKEA goods that three people were crushed to death in Saudi

Arabia in 2004 when IKEA offered a limited number of free $150 vouchers. And when a new IKEA store opened in Edmonton, North London, on 10 February 2005, some 6,000 people turned up . . . at midnight. That's almost as many as watched Davina McCall's primetime chat show. On the Internet, fansites and forums have been set up to discuss the latest IKEA products and how to assemble them in under a week and without losing more than one finger.

Jealous rivals have sniped that IKEA appear to be taking over the world, but would that be such a bad thing? If IKEA had designed Man, maybe his brain would have been put in the right place instead of around the groin area. A trip to IKEA is something that everyone should experience once in their life, rather like skydiving and stewed prunes. With IKEA stores operating a one-way system, which is more rigorously enforced than those in most city centres, there is no danger of getting lost and having to spend the

How to assemble the cupboard

night amid stacks of shelves. Compare this with some Debenhams' stores, which are like Hampton Court Maze. Teenage boys have been known to go in to Debenhams for a pair of trainers and come out with a full beard. With IKEA, everything is orderly, as you would expect from the Swedes. The demand for self-assembly furniture and kitchen accessories shows no sign of abating. May the faucet be with you.

INFLATABLE DOLLS

It is a sad indictment of the world in which we live that it is no longer considered acceptable to take an inflatable woman to a smart restaurant. Turn up at the Savoy Grill with Blow-Up Bertha on your arm and the chances are that you will be politely asked to leave. Yet an inflatable woman can be your best friend – in fact very often your only friend. She always has a nice smile on her face, she doesn't nag, she never has headaches, and she can cope with just about anything except sharp objects. She doesn't spend ages in the bathroom washing her hair, she's a cheap date, and she doesn't have a mother. She's never too tired for sex, she doesn't demand any foreplay, and she doesn't consider premature ejaculation to be a problem. Of course, not everything is perfect. There are one or two drawbacks to an inflatable woman. She tends to go down on you, but not necessarily in the way you want, she can develop alarming wrinkles if she gets too close to the fire, and if she goes on top outdoors on a windy day, there is a very real danger that you might never see her again.

J

JEHOVAH'S WITNESSES

You have to feel sorry for Jehovah's Witnesses. Although there are 6.6 million of them around the world, they always look so lost. This is probably because they are about as welcome in most homes as an infestation of death-watch beetle or a Foster and Allen CD. They must end up with fewer conversions than the England rugby team. But no matter how brusque you are when sending them on their way, they are unfailingly polite. They either just shuffle away dejectedly or thank you for your time when you haven't given them any. Perhaps they are being ironic, but somehow you get the feeling that anyone who can traipse from door to door for hours on end peddling a product that nobody wants, isn't blessed with a particularly well-developed sense of irony. However, whilst being a Jehovah's Witness in the field may seem on a par with selling pork chops in Tel Aviv, there are some perks to the job:

- You get to wear black every day.
- You get *Watchtower* free.
- You'll be the first to hear about the Second Coming.
- You never have to give blood.
- You never have to eat black pudding.
- You never lose any money gambling.

- You get a nice briefcase.
- You never have to walk quickly.
- You get to go everywhere in pairs.

And anyway, compared to most characters that roam the streets, Jehovah's Witnesses are harmless. They don't mug old ladies, they don't try to replace guttering that is in perfectly good condition, and they don't offer to tarmac your drive while reading excerpts from the Old Testament. You simply don't get cowboy religious zealots. So embrace them, invite them into your home for a friendly chat and if they threaten to outstay their welcome, set the dogs on them.

JOB INTERVIEWS

Some people are terrified by job interviews, but they can provide enormous entertainment as they offer you the chance to express yourself in an uninhibited manner. However, if you really want the job, it's probably best to avoid saying any of the following to your prospective employer:

- 'This place is supposed to be a cushy number, right?'
- 'I never work afternoons – I'm too drunk.'
- 'Yes, you can call me Mike, but I'm known as Michaela at weekends.'
- 'The last job I had, I walked out with 80 grand in compensation for wrongful dismissal.'
- 'Which route do your cashiers take to the bank?'
- 'I want your job.'

Waiting for the interview enables you to psyche out

your fellow candidates. Comments such as 'Don't you think that dress is a little too revealing?', 'That colour doesn't suit many people but I think you've just about managed to carry it off' or 'I've heard she's a lesbian' should prove sufficiently unsettling. The wait may also allow you to learn all about the care of office plants, particularly how to revive them after dosing them with the sludge-like contents of the coffee machine. Finally, job interviews give you the opportunity to establish your true worth. This may or may not be a good thing.

JOB TITLES

It's a known fact that the longer the job title, the more insignificant the job. But some of the new politically correct job titles at least carry a degree of self-esteem. Who wouldn't rather be known as a domestic-refusal disposal operative than a binman? Or a customer service representative (cashier)? Or sex worker (prostitute)? From that title, she could just as easily be involved in the pharmaceutical preparation of stimulant gels as giving cut-price blow jobs down a dark alley.

JOGGING

Jogging is supposed to be good for you, but given that Jim Fixx, the guy who pioneered it, dropped dead from a massive heart attack after his daily run at the age of just fifty-two, the benefits must be questionable. Besides, when did you last see a healthy-looking jogger? They always appear to be a split second away from a coronary. So why do they do it? There are easier, less dangerous ways of exercising, such as plucking your eyebrows. As Victoria Wood once remarked: 'Jogging is for people who aren't intelligent enough to watch breakfast television.'

But I do accept that there are plus points to jogging . . . usually provided somebody else is doing it:

- You get to run through other people's picnics without having to apologize.
- No one has ever been delayed on the way to work by a bottleneck of joggers.
- You can get up close and personal with cows.

- You can drink and jog.
- You don't have to take your running shoes in for an MOT.
- You can lap mobility scooters.
- You are an irresistible attraction to large dogs.
- You never have to hold gates open for people.
- If one jogger accidentally bumps into another, it doesn't cause a ten-mile tailback.
- You are often the first to know of any landmines in the area.

JORDAN

Jordan (the model, not the country) has been pilloried for her breast implants and her lifestyle. OK, so she's (allegedly) slept with one or two footballers. What's the big deal? By screwing the Premiership she's only doing what the Premiership has done to fans for the last fifteen years. In reinventing herself as Katie Price, she has demonstrated her intention to remain grounded, a quest in which she is aided by her size

34FF cups. These may appear excessively large and a danger to passing traffic but they are also environmentally friendly as they can provide warmth for at least half a dozen hibernating hedgehogs in winter. Katie may have failed in her bid to represent the UK at the 2005 Eurovision Song Contest, but this should not be taken in isolation: she has failed at lots of things. Besides, there aren't many people who can say they have finished second to Javine at anything. Katie's detractors have accused her of being obsessed with celebrity and of only dating famous, talented people but she has disproved that theory conclusively by marrying Peter Andre. The woman is a saint.

JOURNALISTS

The general perception of a journalist is that of a cross between a leech and a piranha, but without the endearing characteristics of either. In television dramas they are depicted as ruthless, unscrupulous individuals who would sell their own grandmother for a scoop on the local flower show. Put more than two journalists together and you have a pack of hounds positively baying for blood. This less than flattering image of journalists has been carefully cultivated by celebrities and politicians who either already have something to hide or are taking precautions in the absolute certainty that they will have something to hide in the future. And it's woefully inaccurate and unfair. At the start of the working day, journalists do not think: 'I'm going to wreck someone's life today.' Instead most have just three things on their mind: doing their expenses, lunch, and going to the pub, the last two activities invariably being combined. If a story happens to fall into their lap in the course of the day, fine – as long as it's not while they're on the way to the pub. They do not, as a rule, eat babies, nor to my knowledge has any journalist declared war illegally. But as long as any crackhead, bonehead or dickhead celebrity or any philandering politician can convince themselves that their downfall was all the fault of the media, then that's all right. When in doubt, blame the press.

JUDGE JOHN DEED

TV critics complain that the series isn't realistic but Judge John Deed is the ultimate superhero. He acts as judge, prosecution and defence in every trial, rights all of society's wrongs and still finds time to bed a string of gorgeous women. He also cuts cholesterol by half and kills 99 per cent of all household germs.

JUNK MAIL

If all the junk mail delivered to the average household in a year were to be converted into an energy source, it would be sufficient to power the whole of New York City for three months. Fact. Well, actually no. But you get the picture. There's a lot of the stuff. And if you're not looking for a bank loan, home insurance, tree feller, or cheese-and-ham pizza with extra pepperoni, the regular bundle through your letterbox can be mildly irritating. But junk mail isn't so bad. At worst, you just stick it straight in the bin for recycling. If you're Billy no-mates, weekly correspondence from a double-glazing company can almost be a welcome social event, giving you delusions of popularity.

And if your name happens to be Thomas Henry Edward Occupier, it will even seem personal. Besides, delivering junk mail gives postmen something to do on a Monday morning and general advertising leaflets are the one thing they can't deliver to the wrong address. And you never know, one month you may actually win that *Reader's Digest* prize draw.

JURY SERVICE

Jury service is not only a duty, it's a pleasure. True, it can be inconvenient in certain circumstances – particularly if you get a trial that drags on for months or if you find a wreath left at your front door – but for most of us it represents a couple of weeks off work, a change of scenery, and the opportunity to witness the legal system in action. You also get to see people whose lives are an even bigger mess than yours – and that's just your fellow jurors. It's a short day (because the judge usually adjourns at four o'clock to get home in time for *Hollyoaks*), you get around an hour and a half for lunch and you have the chance to make life-changing decisions. Think of a guilty verdict as being like voting off a housemate on *Big Brother*, except that it doesn't cost you £25 a minute.

K

KARAOKE

Karaoke machines are magical contraptions. How else can you explain the fact that the most tone-deaf woman can stand in front of one and immediately think she's Gloria Gaynor? With a voice that could cause a simultaneous avalanche in three different mountain ranges, she bellows out 'I Will Survive', which is more than the tune does. Men on karaoke nights all seem to think they're Robbie Williams, although unfortunately most of them sound more like Kenneth Williams. The only note they can hold is a fiver at the bar.

Although these machines are the bane of many a pub, karaoke is a thoroughly enjoyable pursuit, especially after a few drinks – in fact *only* after a few drinks. If Uncle Les feels like Sinatra or Elvis just for three minutes, it's three minutes when he hasn't been moaning about the price of a pint, telling all and sundry about his enlarged prostate or going on about how badly United are doing. Performing karaoke can also enhance reading skills. A 2006 survey by the Department of Education found that repeating the lyrics from an autocue of favourites like Abba's 'Dancing Queen' or 'Summer Lovin'' from *Grease* requires the reading skills of an eleven-year-old, which is apparently beyond the capabilities of 5.2 million adult Britons. Worse still, those tackling 'I Will Survive' or Robbie Williams's 'Angels' need the reading ability required to pass five good GCSEs, which means that 17.8 million adults wouldn't be able to follow either of those songs. So unless they want to spend the rest of their lives singing The Beatles's 'Ob-La-Di, Ob-La-Da', karaoke presents a perfect incentive for them to brush up on their reading.

PAUL KEATING

Derided for being arrogant and abrasive, Paul Keating was Prime Minister of Australia between 1991 and 1996. He made a number of enemies but nobody could dispute that his colourful turns of phrase livened up the Australian political scene. Now as correspondents witness the polite exchanges that have become the norm in Canberra, they hanker for the good old days when Keating let rip like a stereotypical Aussie. Sir Les Patterson would have been proud of him.

Keating variously described the opposition Liberal Party as 'pansies', 'clowns', 'scumbags', 'cheats', 'frauds', 'mugs', 'dullards', 'dimwits', 'intellectual hoboes', 'blockheads', 'cowboys' and 'dummies', but reserved his finest put-downs for individuals:

- (to Malcolm Fraser) 'You look like an Easter Island statue with an arse full of razor blades.'
- (on John Howard) 'What we have got is a dead carcass, swinging in the breeze, but nobody will cut it down to replace him.'
- (on John Howard) 'I am not like the Leader of the Opposition. I did not slither out of the Cabinet room like a mangy maggot.'
- (on John Howard) 'He is the greatest job and investment

destroyer since the bubonic plague.'

- 'John Howard has more hide than a team of elephants.'
- (on John Hewson) 'Like a lizard on a rock – alive, but looking dead.'
- (on John Hewson) 'He's like a stone statue in the cemetery.'
- Keating called Andrew Peacock 'a gutless spiv' and 'a painted, perfumed gigolo', adding: 'The Liberal Party ought to put him down like a faithful dog because he is of no use to it and of no use to the nation.'
- 'Mike Codd will be lucky to get a job cleaning shithouses if I ever become Prime Minister.'

It's the way he tells them.

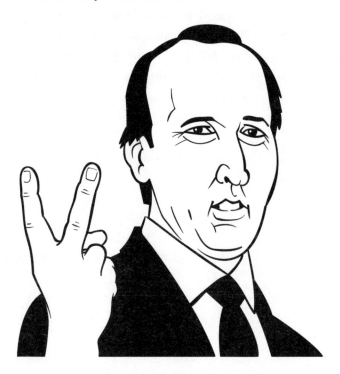

TEDDY KENNEDY

He may be criticised for embracing left-wing ideals, but, unlike most of his family, he's still alive and he has also stopped giving lifts.

KERPLUNK

Why do people get so tense and wound up during a game of KerPlunk? It's one thing to worry about your hand shaking while you're performing open-heart surgery, but the worst that can happen here is a few marbles will fall to the bottom of a plastic container. It's not exactly a matter of life and death. Instead treat KerPlunk for what it is – just about the most fun you can have with marbles . . . apart from swapping one for Grandad's glass eye while he's asleep and then watching him crash into the furniture.

L

LAVA LAMPS

They can lend a sense of nostalgia to your home and in some respects lava lamps are like men – fun to look at but not very bright.

THE LIB DEMS

The Liberal Democrats aren't even the bridesmaids of British politics. They are so distant from the main action that their status is more like that of the florist who arranges the bouquet. But whatever you say about their MPs (or lack of them) and policies (or lack of them), the Lib Dems do a damned good scandal.

In 2006, the party was thrown into turmoil by an unexpected leadership contest. Charles Kennedy was forced to step down, never an easy task for him, as it became clear that scotch and ginger didn't just refer to his nationality and hair colour. Mark Oaten was considered a more sober candidate until it was revealed that he had betrayed his wife and children by having an affair with a rent boy. Next up was Simon Hughes, but he, too, was forced to acknowledge his homosexuality despite having repeatedly denied it in the past. So the top job went to virtually the last man standing, the venerable Ming Campbell, who not only looks as if he

could have served under Gladstone, but also looks like someone for whom any scandal – indeed too much excitement – could well prove fatal.

One consistent factor during the round of leadership exposés was the appearance of the party's only other recognisable figure, the human anagram, Lembit Opik, who was wheeled out to defend his colleagues at every turn. Opik's sole claim to fame, apart from having a name that is one of a kind on Google, was that he was the partner of TV weather forecaster Siân Lloyd. Then, shortly before Christmas, it emerged that he himself was involved in a scandal and had been cheating on Lloyd with singer

Gabriela Irimia, one half of Romania's major contribution to the entertainment industry, The Cheeky Girls. Gabriela, who happens to be half Lloyd's age, is of course fondly remembered for the hit she and identical twin Monica had in 2002 with 'Cheeky Song (Touch My Bum)'. Follow-ups included 'Hooray Hooray (It's a Cheeky Holiday)', 'Have a Cheeky Christmas' and 'Cheeky Flamenco'. In a nutshell, they're cheeky.

Indeed, this latest tale of political debauchery has firmly cemented the Lib Dems as Britain's cheeky party. And how we need them as a contrast to New Labour MPs (whom we try to forget) and Tory MPs (whom we can never remember in the first place). Amid the grey and faceless world of British politics, the Lib Dems stand out for their unashamed sense of fun and adventure. Jeremy Thorpe must be so proud of them.

LIES

Big lies are, of course, utterly reprehensible (unless they happen to save your skin) but in certain circumstances little white lies are excusable, even advisable. For example:

- Officer, I only had two beers.
- This won't hurt.
- I'll give you a call.
- Your bum doesn't look big.
- Tell me. I promise I won't get angry.
- We've had a lot of interest in this property.
- He's just a friend.
- It was delicious, you must give me the recipe.

- Then take a left, you can't miss it.
- Of course it was good for me.
- I never received your invoice.
- I've never done anything like this before.
- Our insurance policy gives you peace of mind.
- I had no idea the pictures would be published.
- The engine's supposed to make that noise.
- It's not the money, it's the principle.
- Don't worry, madam, the sleeves will ride up with wear.
- I'll respect you in the morning.

LIFE COACHES

'Life is like a river. It's moving, and you can be at the mercy of the river if you fail to take deliberate, conscious action to steer yourself in a direction you have predetermined.' These are the words of American life coach Tony Robbins, who is basically saying you need to plan ahead. Pretty standard really, except that life coaches can charge hundreds of dollars for stating the bleeding obvious. Under no circumstances should a life coach be confused with a lifeguard. If you get into difficulties while swimming in the sea, a life coach will not come to your rescue. He or she will, however, be able to advise on where is best to hold the funeral.

Life coaches seem superfluous to those of us who think we are perfectly capable of running our own lives, but maybe there is something to be said for them. If Napoleon had employed a life coach, he would never have set foot anywhere near Moscow. A life coach would have advised the Big Bad Wolf of the futility of trying to blow down a house made of brick. A life coach might even have encouraged Tony Blair to stick with the music and not go into politics. So don't knock them.

LOCAL TV NEWS

There is always something quaintly reassuring about local TV news. Perhaps it's the forced chemistry of the presenters. They appear all matey, even flirtatious, on screen, but you know that as soon as the end credits roll, they are bitching over everything, from who talked over the other's introduction to which of them ate the last Rich Tea. Even married presenters have probably taken out restraining

orders on each other. Or maybe it's the disappointment etched on their faces when reporting a house fire in which no one was actually hurt, although to make the incident seem more dramatic they invariably slip in the stock phrase 'It's a miracle no one was killed.' Perhaps it's the desperate attempts to work a local angle into a major national story – 'Glossop man once visited World Trade Center' or 'Accrington woman met man at bus stop who said he knew Gordon Brown'. If there had been regional TV news when the *Titanic* went down, it would have kept them going for months. Or maybe it's the compulsory jolly banter with the weather presenter who is either a wannabe starlet who thinks an occluded front is like a halterneck, or a guy with shoulders so broad that they obscure half of the weather map. There have been people in parts of the West Midlands who haven't had any weather for months.

Local TV news has also been almost singlehandedly responsible for prolonging the career of dear old Denis Norden. For whenever *It'll Be Alright On The Night* ran out of achingly dull bloopers from celebrities and soaps, it could always fall back on a plentiful supply of outtakes from the world's local news programmes, usually involving a pert blonde reporter and a vengeful cow.

LOGARITHMS

What were they all about? We devoted so much time to them in maths lessons that they must be important. Then again we did a lot of algebra and the only use I can see for that is working out what Coldplay's 2005 album added up to. Apparently logarithms did serve a purpose, however, because complicated multiplication and division could be simplified by using tables of logarithms and antilogarithms. 'For example,' explains the Hutchinson Encyclopedia, 'to multiply 6,560 by 980, one looks up their logarithms (3.8169 and 2.9912) adds them together (6.8081), then looks up the antilogarithm of this to get the answer (6,428,800).' Similarly if you want to find out which pope reigned between Gregory XI and Boniface IX, look up their respective dates (1370 and 1389), look up the date of the nearest antipope (Clement VII, 1378), match that date with the list of popes and you have the answer (Urban VI).

What could be simpler? But now cheap electronic calculators do the job instead. If you ask me, it's just another example of dumbing down. Bring back logarithms. You can calculate 5 x 5 in just eighteen easy stages. John Napier didn't invent them just for fun, you know. It must have taken him years to work out all those tables. I'm sure he had better things to do with his time. And all to be replaced by a £2.99 calculator.

LOUD SHIRTS

Loud shirts don't just say something about a man, they scream it. Generally, Hawaiian shirts are fine in Honolulu, but not so good in Wigan. The clue is in the name really. Yet even if worn outside their natural habitat, loud shirts perform a valuable social function. Just as the skunk has its foul spray and a rattlesnake has its rattle, so a loud shirt warns you that the wearer is someone to be avoided at all costs. Loud shirts are also good for concealing all manner of stains, from barbecue sauce to beetroot. You simply pass them off as part of the pattern. So don't let the government push ahead with its plans to ban loud shirts in built-up areas between 9 p.m. and 9 a.m. It must be an infringement of human rights. Everything else seems to be.

LUTON

Whenever there's a poll to determine the worst town or city in the world to live, Luton can be relied upon to give Baghdad and Beirut a run for their money. 'Dreary, concrete and polluted' was one of the more polite descriptions of the place. In its defence, the town has had a troubled history. It was heavily bombed by the Germans during the Second World War, reducing entire streets to rubble, although nobody actually noticed until 1959. If the Luftwaffe were to return today, it could cause thousands of pounds worth of improvements. Then, in 2002, one of the town's great tourist attractions, the Vauxhall Motors Factory, closed. But all is not lost. There is still the Arndale Centre, as well as the site of a factory that once made ball bearings, not to mention the town hall, which boasts the heaviest bell in the whole of Bedfordshire. If these three attractions aren't enough to have busloads of Japanese tourists flocking to Luton, there is simply no pleasing some people. And let's not forget that Diana Dors once worked as a barmaid in a pub in Luton. Of course, the pub

is no longer there. Luton may not be the prettiest of towns – more egg box than chocolate box – but dozens of muggers are happy to call it home. But, without a doubt, the best thing about Luton is its excellent transport links – the railway, the M1 motorway and the airport – because if you do live there, the most important thing is to be able to get out of the place as quickly as possible.

LUVVIES

They live in their own little world where the air is rarefied. They are not bred to cope with everyday life, with the result that they can turn a faulty stopcock or a broken fingernail into a drama straight from *King Lear*. If you happen to come across a luvvie, remember they are delicate souls with fragile egos, and that every conversation is an audition. But luvvies are essentially harmless and we love them almost as much as they love themselves. If luvvies ruled the world there would be no wars, no bigotry, and any threat to the future of the planet would be erased on the second draft.

M

MARMITE

You either love it or hate it. Well, that's what the advertisers say, although there must be thousands of people in the world who remain blissfully indifferent towards Marmite. Back in the 1930s, the product's advertising revolved around its alleged ability to repair a broken marriage. A character called Ma Marmite – the Claire Rayner of her day – told magazine readers: 'If every married woman could make really good hash, there'd be fewer hashes made of marriage. That's why I say – always have a jar of Marmite at hand.' Since then the divorce rate has risen while Marmite's popularity has declined. Coincidence?

Marmite's high Vitamin B content has also made it highly prized by the medical profession. In the early 1950s, a special booklet was produced extolling the remedial virtues of the famous yeast extract and revealing that it was considered efficacious for diabetes, ulcers, rheumatism and nervous and mental complaints. Stranger still, Marmite was once prescribed in the Eastern tropics to cure burning feet and beriberi, and the Medical Research Council's 1951 report on 'Deficiency Diseases in Japanese Prison Camps' stated that Marmite had proved effective in the treatment of scrotal dermatitis. The report did not indicate whether the Marmite was meant to be taken orally or applied to the affected parts but presumably the patients were the original 'Marmite soldiers'.

So there you have it. Marmite saves marriages and cures rheumatism and itchy bollocks. You don't get that with an Oxo cube.

ANN MAURICE

The American rottweiler of soft furnishings may not be everyone's favourite style guru but nobody can accuse her of mincing her words. She doesn't sit on the fence, she demolishes it. She makes Ruby Wax look like a shrinking violet. But although a visit from 'House Doctor' Ann creates a sensation not unlike having an entire Panzer division crashing through your front door, she does talk a lot of sense. She only bullies homeowners because some of them have such appalling taste. If you model your lounge colour scheme on a margherita pizza, you deserve to be criticised. If you think that a full-size stuffed orang-utan makes an entertaining focal point in the main bedroom, accept that Ann may not agree with you. And if your dining room is cluttered with eighty-three brightly-coloured plastic bullfrogs in a range of appealing poses, Ann is perfectly within her rights to point out that you may have difficulty selling your house.

As a result of the inevitable conflicts, her TV show is extremely watchable, albeit nervously from behind a cushion . . . which Ann would say is in the wrong place anyway. And remember, all the time she's at someone else's house, it means she's not at yours.

MODERN ART

When Emmanuel Asare, a cleaner at a London art gallery, spotted a pile of full ashtrays, beer bottles, cola cans, coffee cups and sweet wrappings, he naturally thought they were leftovers from a party. So he dumped the lot in a bin, only to discover that the 'rubbish' was a £5,000 work of art by Damien Hirst. The cleaner's blunder was perfectly understandable because Hirst is the man who has introduced the art world to the joys of, among other

things, a shark in formaldehyde, a rotting cow's head covered in maggots and flies, and a pickled sheep in a tank. He probably had to get the sheep drunk to persuade it to take part.

Many people dismiss these and other modern exhibits such as Tracey Emin's notorious unmade bed (which appeared complete with used condoms and bloodstained underwear) as a waste of time and space. And they could well be right. But modern art does open up possible solutions to modern ills. For example if you came across a dead sheep lying in the middle of the High Street, normally you wouldn't know what to do with it. Now the answer is simple: put the sheep in a large jiffy bag and send it to your nearest artist-in-residence. He or she will be sure to put it to good use. Next time you go to a refuse tip, instead of grimacing at the pile of old sofas, broken chairs and rusty beds, stop for a moment and consider that you could be looking at a future Turner Prize winner. Similarly when you walk through the old chicken bones, cigarette packs and beer cans that litter most city streets, think that in the right hands they could fetch £10,000.

That's the thing with modern art: nothing is ugly. Everything is beautiful and has a purpose. In time it would be nice to think that we could do away with street cleaners altogether and just have gangs of artists and sculptors patrolling our towns and cities collecting discarded items for their works, like latter-day Wombles. Council Tax bills would be reduced instantly. And it would all be down to modern art.

MONDAYS

As the start of the working week, Monday is traditionally the most miserable of days. That Monday morning feeling as we trek into the office tends to extend through the rest of the day. Statistics show that more people commit suicide on a Monday than any other day of the week and that Monday is also the most common day for suffering a heart attack. Car breakdowns and teenage migraines are most frequent on a Monday, which is apparently also the least successful day for job applicants. And in 1979, sixteen-year-old Brenda Spencer opened fire on San Diego schoolchildren because 'I don't like Mondays.' This tragedy was all the worse for inadvertently boosting Bob Geldof's musical career.

But are Mondays really all doom and gloom? Well, there are two episodes of *Coronation Street* in the evening as opposed to only one of *EastEnders*, so that's a reason to be cheerful. And nobody expects you to socialise on a Monday evening, so if your life is empty, you're not missing out on anything. Anyway, other days aren't necessarily bundles of fun either. Friday – quite apart from the misfortunes associated with the 13th – is the worst day for road accidents and bank robberies, Tuesday is the least popular day for sex, and Thursday is the worst day to be admitted to hospital (because with consultants not working weekends, you'll still be there at the start of the following week). Wonderful things have happened on Mondays. John Paul II became Pope on a Monday (16 October, 1978). There must be others.

MORRIS DANCING

In rural England, some folk play rugby, some play football, and others dance around waving sticks and handkerchiefs while dressed in funny costumes with bells on. The ancient ritual of morris dancing might not appear to be the most macho pursuit, but some of these men are hardened drinkers, capable of holding their own at the bar with any prop forward. Tapping sticks in unison obviously builds up quite a thirst.

Morris dancing may appear easy, but each step is carefully choreographed with an attention to detail that makes Take That look like amateurs. Mercifully, for the sake of nervous spinsters and local livestock, morris

SMOKING
ALARM

FIRE

MORRIS
DANCERS
ALARM

dancers do, however, refrain from baring their chests during a performance. Morris dancers drive out evil spirits, offer a positive, athletic outlet for those who might otherwise be subject to Care in the Community schemes, and provide a colourful spectacle in areas where the only other modern tradition is joyriding. But the best thing about morris dancers is that with all their bells, you can hear them coming a mile off and so have plenty of time to escape to the next village.

MOSQUITOES

It's only the females that suck blood, so really mosquitoes aren't much different to humans.

JOSÉ MOURINHO

The Chelsea Football Club manager sees himself as the 'Special One'. So modesty may not exactly be his strong point but if you've got it, flaunt it. Few of the most successful managers have been self-effacing (you could never describe Bill Shankly or Brian Clough as shy and retiring), and while there are modest managers in football, that is usually because they have much to be modest about. Mourinho has been a much-needed breath of fresh air in the Premiership, and women love him. If you were on *Blind Date* and had to choose between Mourinho, Sir Alex Ferguson and Rafa Benitez, you wouldn't need Alan Hansen to predict the result. So, criticise the Chelsea manager? No way, José.

THE MULLET

As a hairstyle (although in this case the word 'style' is used loosely), the mullet has long attracted ridicule. David Bowie was one of the pioneers of the mullet before it was copied with distinction by the likes of Chris Waddle, Michael Bolton, Billy Ray Cyrus, Paul Calf and Pat Sharp. Indeed, the last-named, an otherwise unremarkable British DJ, was known almost solely for his mullet, which made him look like Lenny the Lion's long-lost brother. This is the point of the mullet: it gives the wearer an identity, in much the same way that the Elephant Man had an identity. Although Sharp's splendid mane appeared to require at least six hours' preparation before he could face his public, Bolton's stragglier design seemed to need little attention. It was virtually ready to wear. It must also have saved him washing his neck for several years.

The mullet has spawned a culture all of its own. Books, websites and appreciation societies have been devoted to the mullet, while Pittsburgh is very nearly proud to call itself the Mullet Capital of America. The mullet has become a worldwide phenomenon, known in different parts of the US as 'The Beaver Paddle', 'The Mississippi Mudflap' and 'The Alabama Shag'. In Australia it is nicknamed 'Freddie Firedrill', because the victim – sorry, customer – supposedly had his haircut interrupted by the sound of a fire alarm after the barber had finished shaving the front of the head, but before he had started on the back. In Canada, it is called 'Hockey Hair', on account of its popularity among ice hockey players; in Denmark it is

referred to as 'Bundesliga Hair', because for an indecent number of years it was the preferred hairstyle among German footballers; and the Greek term is 'Laspotiras', which appropriately means 'mudflap'. The Japanese call it 'Wolf Hair', the Turks describe it as 'Lion's Mane', and the Serbian term for the mullet is 'Tarzanka', in honour of Tarzan the Ape Man. There is even a spin-off style, the 'skullet', which combines a bald head with long hair down the back, the thinking perhaps being that when it reaches the base of the spine it can be gathered up to form the ultimate comb-over. Think comedian Bill Bailey, American actor Dennis Franz or wildlife presenter Terry

Nutkins whose flowing locks are thought to serve as a nesting box for over a dozen species of bird.

Although sadly the mullet has died out in many parts of the world, there are still breeding colonies in Germany and Austria. It is comforting to know that this most distinctive of hairstyles has not been completely lost.

MUZAK

Piped music is a wonderful concept. Who cannot say that a fifty-minute wait to get through to an insurance company's call centre hasn't been made infinitely more bearable by listening to a loop of *The Best of James Last*? Or that an afternoon of arduous Christmas shopping hasn't been turned into a thoroughly joyous occasion by the sound of 'Santa Claus Is Coming To Town' playing in every store you visit? And if you're trapped in an elevator, fast running out of oxygen and with no chance of being rescued, what better way to spend your dying moments than by trying to work out whether the muzak you're hearing is 'Edelweiss' or 'Stairway to Heaven'?

MUZZLED POLICE DOGS

These days the words 'police initiative' carry an immediate sense of foreboding, unless of course you happen to be a criminal. Every new idea dreamed up by British police forces seems designed to protect their officers from the risk of injury, litigation or nasty name-calling while making life easier for villains. In some rural areas police officers will no longer make foot patrols down narrow lanes because it is considered too dangerous and anyway they might get mud splattered up their nice new uniforms. Instead they prefer to stay in the warmth of the station and concentrate on paperwork, with full medical back-up and legal advice in place in case they sustain any career-threatening paper cuts. It brings a whole new meaning to 'police protection'.

Just when it seemed that public confidence in the police was at an all-time low, North Wales Police managed to plumb new depths by announcing that in future their police dogs would be muzzled to stop them injuring criminals. Following a rise in the number of compensation claims from suspects bitten by police dogs, Chief Constable Richard Brunstrom revealed that animals were being trained to disable their targets with flying head-butts instead. Brunstrom's obsession with trapping speeding motorists has led to him reportedly encouraging officers to hide behind walls and road signs with handheld devices. Had he been around in Roman times, he would probably have had Ben Hur thrown to the lions while letting the murderous Caligula off with a caution.

On the face of it, a toothless police dog appears no more of a weapon in the fight against crime than a plasticine baton or paper handcuffs. If the police are concerned about criminals being hurt, why not employ less savage breeds of dog, like a papillon or maybe a Yorkshire terrier wearing a nice black-and-white checked bow on its head? If nothing else, the ignominy of a burly armed robber being arrested by a police papillon would be enough to make him go straight for the rest of his life. The practicality of head-butting is also unclear. The dogs, which are believed to be trained by watching videos of Zinedine Zidane at the 2006 World Cup, apparently need a long, clear run-up before being able to launch themselves with sufficient force to be effective. It follows that for the tactic to work, the suspect needs to be both stupid and immobile – stupid enough not to realise that an Alsatian wearing running spikes and coming at him from thirty yards with a homicidal look in its eye is a serious threat, and immobile enough not to be able to take the step to the left or right that would see the flying dog disappear into the nearest hedge. Isn't there also a risk that all those blows to the head could result in police dogs ending up punch-drunk like boxers? Pensioned off from the force for head-butting a patrol car, Rex would spend his last lonely days in a dogs' home chasing his own tail and telling fellow residents that he was really Sir Ian Blair.

But while the plan to muzzle police dogs may sound barking mad, consider the plus points:

- Police dogs would no longer need expensive dental check-ups.
- Gum disease would not be a bar to a dog joining the police force.
- Criminals could not demand compensation for being traumatised by unpleasant dog breath.
- Fractured ribs are cheaper to treat than rabies.
- A display team of flying dogs – maybe called the Red Rovers – would prove a popular addition to Crufts.

So that's settled. All police dogs should be muzzled, and while we're at it, let's also muzzle Chief Constables.

N

NAVEL FLUFF

It's one of life's great mysteries: how does all that fluff congregate in men's navels? Why doesn't it collect anywhere else on the body? And why doesn't it match the colour of the clothes they've been wearing? Navel fluff may seem like one of the world's most worthless and pointless commodities, but try telling that to Australian Graham Barker who has earned a place in Guinness World Records for having the world's largest collection of navel fluff. He started collecting navel fluff (and only ever his own) back in 1984 in the hope of eventually amassing sufficient to stuff a cushion. His daily harvest reaps an average of 3.03 milligrams – collected over twenty years this is enough to fill more than two large jars but not yet enough to stuff that cushion.

On his website, The Incredible World of Navel Fluff, Barker reveals his fascination for collecting his belly button lint. For a start, he says his collection is unique – as far as he knows, nobody else collects navel fluff. Who knows, there may be cheap imitators out there but no one can dispute that when it comes to navel fluff, Graham Barker is the daddy. Secondly, he points out that his collection has that priceless quality – rarity. 'The navel fluff of Graham Barker is produced in very limited qualities by only one person,' he says, 'and is not easily obtainable by others.' Thirdly, having seldom missed a day's fluff harvest over the past twenty-three years, he believes his collection to be almost complete, like having the full set of a country's currency. Lastly, he states that, like uncirculated banknotes or stamps, his navel fluff is in mint condition. 'When harvested, I remove any body hair from the fluff then store it immediately in a jar, where it remains uncontaminated.'

As well as outlining the joys of navel fluff, Barker has undertaken invaluable research to improve our understanding of it. He confirms the widely held belief that navel fluff forms when tiny pieces of fibre break off the inside of clothing. Although women do acquire navel fluff, more accumulates on overweight men because they have deeper belly buttons and hairier stomachs. Abdominal hair dislodges fibres from clothes and also channels the fibres into the navel. So if you want to get lint, get a beer gut. It has also been suggested that navels may possess a moist and sticky secretion that catches whatever lands nearby, rather like the inside of a carnivorous plant. Rest assured, however, that gentle digital probing of your navel is unlikely to result in an emergency call to the fire brigade to free your finger. Regarding the colour, Barker quotes American navel fluff expert Michael Biesecker who has observed that those who habitually wear clothes of a similar colour tend to produce lint of that colour. However, those who wear a variety of colours often end up with greyish-blue fluff, as in the filters of washing machines and tumble driers. This, it is thought, represents an average of all clothing colours worn. Still doesn't explain my navy blue.

So you should never take navel fluff for granted. It is undemanding, user-friendly and, as Graham Barker has shown, can provide a rewarding and stimulating hobby. There's a whole new world down there just waiting to be explored.

NEIGHBOURS

Its critics say it isn't Shakespeare, but neither is it *Love Island*, *I'm A Celebrity Get Me Out Of Here*, *The Paul O'Grady Show*, *Wife Swap*, *Celebrity Fit Club* or anything

with Vanessa Feltz. On that basis alone, it deserves to run for at least another twenty glorious years, by which time Karl Kennedy will have discovered a cure for cancer, he and Susan will have remarried for a fourth time, Harold and Lou will have become an item, and Bouncer's long-lost, illegitimate grandpuppies will have returned to wreak havoc on Ramsay Street.

SAPARMURAT NIYAZOV

Maybe he could be a touch dictatorial at times but nobody could accuse the former President of Turkmenistan of not knowing his own mind. Sensing that his country lacked an identity, he decided to lend it his. He renamed a major town, several schools, airports, a meteorite, the months of the year and the days of the week after himself and his family, thereby making it simpler for his subjects to remember things. He closed all rural libraries on the grounds that villagers didn't read books and he ensured that any textbooks that did exist contained his personal version of history. This was enormously beneficial as it saved his people having to think for themselves. Niyazov's face appeared on the nation's banknotes and he had large portraits of himself hung all over Turkmenistan. Statues of himself and his mother were also scattered liberally, including a gold-plated one on top of Ashgabat's tallest building, the Neutrality Arch, that rotated to face the sun and thereby shone constant light into the capital city. Bearing in mind that failure to recognize the President was liable to result in imprisonment or exile, it was essential to have reminders of his face on every corner. 'I'm personally against seeing my pictures and statues in the streets,' he remarked modestly, 'but it's what the people want.'

While Tony Blair's endless gimmicks have singularly failed to improve the behaviour of Britain's teenagers, Niyazov tackled the youth culture problem with typical gusto. He banned young men from wearing long hair or beards, he banned them from getting gold teeth, and he banned them from playing video games. He also banned ballet and opera, car radios, and something that is seen by academics as being one of the major causes of youthful discontent and rebellion across the world – lip-synching. In 2004, he banned newsreaders from wearing make-up because he was having difficulty telling male and female presenters apart. Who hasn't had the same problem with Huw Edwards and Fiona Bruce? When it came to cleaning up the capital, Niyazov's solution was simple, straightforward and a lesson to other world leaders: he banned dogs. He didn't like them much anyway.

Forget Gerald Ford, forget Charlie Drake, Saparmurat Niyazov's death was the greatest loss of Christmas 2006. He will be sorely missed.

NODDY

In more than fifty years of living in Toytown, Noddy has been accused of numerous 'crimes' against humanity. He has been branded a middle-class snob and labelled homosexual, racist, and cruel to people with disabilities.

His chief tormentors were the black-skinned golliwogs of Golly Town who served as Toytown's criminal element and who once stole Noddy's beloved car. Perceived as racist, the golliwogs were replaced by goblins in 1989, only for Scandinavian countries to protest that their trolls were being insulted. To cement Noddy's new enlightened attitude, in 1992 the BBC introduced Dinah Doll, 'a black, assertive minority female'.

Noddy's friendship with Big Ears has regularly prompted raised eyebrows but there is no evidence in the stories to suggest that the relationship was in any way physical. Despite the size of his friend's ears, there is not even a hint of aural sex. Naturally, Big Ears was renamed Whitebeard for the US market because ultra-sensitive Americans wouldn't dream of giving a character with extra large ears an insulting name, like, say, Dumbo.

Noddy's middle-class mindset has softened in recent years, although not to the extent that he has taken to calling Mr Tubby Bear 'dude'. Nor does he mock with the same ferocity the physically challenged Mr Wobbly Man who, sadly, is unable to lie down because of his wobbler. (If you have been affected by any of the issues that concern Mr Wobbly Man, there is a helpline you can ring at the end of the programme.) Also, Noddy no longer lends his unconditional support to the fascist Mr Plod the policeman, although the latter is now too busy dealing with Home Office paperwork to nick criminals.

So give Noddy a break. The poor guy has spent his whole life walking around with a bell on his hat. Hasn't he suffered enough? Besides, he has plenty of famous fans including Jack Nicholson, Lisa Kudrow, Jonathan Ross and Ronan Keating. Incidentally, in Germany Noddy is known as Purzelknirps. Makes you think, doesn't it?

O

OBESITY

It's an accepted medical fact that fat people are jolly, and small people are obnoxious. On the one hand you have Oliver Hardy, Harry Secombe, Christopher Biggins; on the other you have Hitler, Napoleon, George W. Bush – all three troublemakers. Having said that, if you were in a hot air balloon with Hitler and Winston Churchill and were rapidly losing altitude, who would you throw out first?

OFFICE CHRISTMAS DINNERS

In many firms the office Christmas dinner is the most dreaded date in the calendar. It's compulsory to attend (even a death certificate isn't sufficient excuse in some companies), you usually have to pay for it out of your own pocket, and all you get for your money is a seat next to someone you've tried to avoid all year and a lukewarm meal consisting of two slices of see-through turkey, a roast potato that's seen better days and a dozen Brussels sprouts that nobody wants, all washed down with the sort of cheap wine that could take the enamel off your teeth. And you're supposed to look as if you're having a wonderful time, even when the CEO makes his speech telling you how much he values you all before casually

mentioning that market forces dictate there will have to be 125 redundancies over the following year.

So what's good about the office Christmas dinner, apart from the fact that it only happens once a year? The key is in the seating arrangements. Either make sure you're sitting next to like-minded souls . . . and slowly get drunk, or seat yourself among the office sycophants who won't touch alcohol for fear of saying the wrong thing to the boss . . . and slowly get drunk. That way you won't give a toss about anyone or anything. Why should you? You're going to be made redundant next year anyway.

OLD BANDS

Look in the 'what's on' section of any local paper, and there between the 'discreet massage for discerning gentlemen' and details of a church-hall flower-arranging competition, you'll find an advert for an old Sixties band like the Swinging Blue Jeans playing at the nearest British Legion. And, partly in a wave of nostalgia, and partly because you've forgotten to take your medication, you buy tickets. But when you arrive, there's only one original band member and he's so fat he has to be winched into his blue jeans. And he's now of an age when he's more likely to poop his pants than swing them. He's joined on stage by a stray Dreamer (who defected after Freddie's death), someone who once knew a Mindbender, and a bloke from the Job Centre. But are you disappointed? No, because they sound better than anybody off any show with Louis Walsh as a judge, they're obviously enjoying themselves (if only because they're grateful still to be alive) and anyway it keeps them off the streets.

P

PANTOMIME

Panto is great. Oh no it isn't! Oh yes it is! You get to boo undesirable individuals without the risk of being arrested by the thought police and you see girls slapping their thighs and grown men dressed as women for a fraction of the price it would cost in Soho.

PARANOIA

A little healthy paranoia is fine. No problem. What are you looking at?

PARKING ATTENDANTS

Every motorist despises traffic wardens, but what would happen without them? Anarchy, that's what. Proof that traffic wardens are a vital cog in the wheel of civilisation occurred shortly before Christmas 2006 when the only warden in the Gloucestershire town of Tewkesbury was suspended from duty, and not, it is believed, because he slapped a ticket on the Chief Constable's car. In his absence, the townsfolk ran amok, parking on double yellow lines without fear of retribution. They were like a bunch of school kids when the teacher is called out of

class. Then it dawned on the traders that, because of vehicles that were triple parked in places, the town centre was gridlocked and nobody was able to use the shops at such a potentially lucrative time of the year. Business plummeted and the traders were hugely relieved when, within a few days, a new warden was imported from another district. Immediately, parking tickets were being issued again and normality was restored.

Traffic wardens are a necessary evil. Left to its own devices, the human race is capable of enormous folly. It has wiped out whole species in the past, so imagine what it could do to a small town High Street. Without traffic wardens, people would simply park anywhere – on pedestrian crossings, in the middle of the road, in the foyer of Barclays Bank – because so many motorists are too lazy to put their legs into gear. Somebody has to keep them in check – and that person is the local traffic warden. And compared to wheel clampers who, if not actually the devil incarnate are surely close relatives, traffic wardens are absolute pussycats. Also, whereas The Beatles penned 'Lovely Rita' in homage to a meter maid, they never wrote a song about florists or cake-shop owners or ice cream vendors. So traffic wardens must have something going for them.

PASSPORT PHOTOS

Have you ever wondered what David Bailey's passport photo looks like? Or Madonna's? They're probably no better than anyone else's, and let's face it, we all hate our passport photos. But think positively. There is a lot to be learned from your passport photo.

- Your passport photo shows you how you will look in twenty years time.
- Your passport photo shows what you would look like if you were a Romanian refugee.
- Your passport photo shows how you would look if you had just drunk a pint of vinegar.
- Your passport photo shows you how you would look on *Crimewatch*.
- Your passport photo shows you how to look when someone informs you of a sudden death in the family.
- Any country that will let you in looking like your passport photo is not worth visiting.

PE TEACHERS

PE teachers are just school bullies without the uniform. Invariably considered too right-wing for the Ku Klux Klan and too sadistic for the SS, they proceed to make life hell for any pupil who doesn't know his Arsenal from the elbow at Aintree. Ironically, PE teachers themselves are hopeless at every known sport, their only apparent qualifications for the job being that they own a tracksuit and know how to blow a whistle. But maybe society has judged PE teachers too harshly. There could be valuable lessons to be learned from them:

- They teach you the art of walking along a ridiculously narrow beam.
- They teach you the art of climbing wall bars and looking petrified when you reach the top.
- They teach you how to react if anyone suddenly throws a medicine ball at you in the street.
- They teach you how to vault over a large wooden box – crucial if your path is ever blocked by a large wooden box.
- They teach you the rules of crab football – essential knowledge if it ever becomes an Olympic sport.
- As the embodiment of ignorance and prejudice, they teach you the importance of a good education.

Also:

- Nobody pays any attention to what PE teachers write on your school report.
- You know they are treated as a joke in the staffroom.
- You know that sooner or later male PE teachers will be sacked for being caught in a compromising position in the stock room with the PE mistress.

PEANUT BUTTER

It may look like something you spread between ceramic kitchen tiles, but you have to put the world's peanut produce to some use. If it weren't for peanut butter, which eats up two-thirds of the US peanut harvest, peanuts would be everywhere. They'd cover streets, driveways, entire neighbourhoods. They'd be all over your lounge, in your bed, and instead of fluff in your belly button you'd find a couple of peanuts.

PENALTY SHOOT-OUTS

'Penalty shoot-outs are soooo unfair!' That's the cry from every football manager who has ever lost one. They're a test of skill (for both the taker and the goalkeeper), they certainly require nerve, and they're a damn sight more entertaining for spectators than watching a coin being tossed. Anyway, what's the alternative? Play on and on through the night in the hope that someone eventually scores a deciding goal? Hold a lovely legs contest among the players, the team with the best pins going through to the next round? Have a pillow fight? Nah. I think we'll stick with penalties.

PLINY THE ELDER

Whaddaguy!

PLUTO

The cruel decision to kick Pluto out of the Solar System (with no right of appeal) has seriously damaged the reputation of the major planets. The official line is that a planet is now being defined as a celestial body that is in orbit around the Sun, has sufficient mass to assume a round shape, and has cleared the neighbourhood around its orbit. Pluto was disqualified on the grounds that its oblong orbit overlaps with Neptune's. So it has been downgraded to the status of 'dwarf planet'. Although astronomers took the rap for Pluto's humiliation, there is a suspicion that the move was orchestrated by the Big Two – Jupiter and Saturn – who are thought to be planning a breakaway Solar System. This theory was reinforced last November when Neptune received a message by rocket warning 'You're next.'

Thankfully, Pluto's seventy-six years of loyal dedication to its fellow planets has not been forgotten, and, in order to ensure its immortality, American language experts have come up with the verb 'to pluto', meaning to demote or devalue someone or something. Indeed the American Dialect Society named 'plutoed' its word of 2006. Society President Cleveland Evans explained: 'Our members believe the great emotional reaction of the public to the demotion of Pluto shows the importance of Pluto as a name.' He went on to reveal that 'plutoed' won in a run-off against 'climate canary' – defined as 'an organism or species whose poor health or declining numbers hint at a larger environmental catastrophe on the horizon.' No contest.

POLITICAL CORRECTNESS

A man is no longer a male chauvinist pig – instead he has swine empathy; he does not fart and belch – instead he is gastronomically expressive; and a woman does not get PMS – she becomes hormonally homicidal. Political correctness. Don't you just love it? Well, actually, yes, because the seemingly unstoppable march of political correctness has brightened up our lives immeasurably by providing an endless source of material for satirists the world over.

Every day brings some crazy new story. A Kent drama group hoping to stage *Snow White And The Seven Dwarfs* for their Christmas panto were stunned when they received the script with the word 'dwarf' censored.

'Three visually impaired rodents'

Instead, Snow White's gang were to be referred to as 'gnomes' or 'guardians of the forest'. In the north-east of England, Geordie council workers were ordered not to call women 'pet' because the traditional greeting was suddenly deemed disrespectful. Instead, females were to be addressed by their full name, and to ensure the message got home, staff were sent on 'equality and diversity' courses. The familiar nursery rhyme 'Baa Baa Black Sheep' was changed at one London nursery school to 'Baa Baa Rainbow Sheep' in order to avoid causing offence, and another school teacher in England suggested banning the use of the word 'fail' in favour of 'deferred success'. So presumably if she teaches history, she doesn't say King Harold failed to beat William the Conqueror at the Battle of Hastings in 1066, it was merely a deferred success. Try telling that to Harold.

In St Albans, West Virginia, officials intended the town's 2006 nativity scene to go ahead without Jesus, Mary or Joseph for fear of upsetting other religions. Following widespread protests (some from as far away as Korea), a baby was reluctantly placed in the manger but Mary and Joseph were nowhere to be seen. Perhaps they still couldn't get a room.

Even Britain's Commission for Racial Equality showed that it saw the funny side of political correctness by distributing an official Christmas card that ridiculed some modern views. The supposed draft card of a standard festive scene contained scribbled suggestions. One said, 'Three wise men can't all be men', and another added, 'The snow looks hideously white.' Pointing to the stable, one comment read: 'Stable not compliant with housing code – where is disabled access?' Highlighting the reindeer, someone wrote, 'Important: Animals pulling sleigh should be product of equal opportunities employment policies, not all one species.' And alongside a flock of black-faced sheep was the remark, 'Sheep should look more diverse!'

We should all be able to laugh at political correctness because a lot of it is one big joke. And the stories it throws up are funnier than stale old jokes about mothers-in-law who are fat . . . sorry, metabolic underachievers.

POODLES

They're yappy, they're vain, they're highly strung – and that's just the owners. They say dog owners gradually start to look like their pets, and that's where poodles come in useful. Because if you start to look like your poodle, you know it's time to find a new hairdresser. A poodle is just a topiary on legs but there's no danger of a poodle owner being prosecuted under the Dangerous Dogs Act as the only time a poodle ever starts frothing at the mouth is if it has accidentally swallowed some of its favourite all-in-one conditioner, moisturiser and bubble bath.

POP UPS

One minute you are merrily surfing the Internet, the next you are suddenly being offered a date with a pneumatic woman of Eastern European origin, whose pose strongly suggests that she does not do platonic. You've had a pop up. In fact if you're a red-blooded man, you've probably had two pop ups simultaneously. On-screen pop ups are considered by many to be the biggest nuisance on the Internet, surpassing even unsolicited penis-enlargement emails or Ask Jeeves, whose answers invariably managed to make the educated butler appear thicker than Bertie Wooster. The most innocuous Google search can trigger them off. 'Great Tit', 'Canadian Beaver' and 'Mutual Masturbation' can all unleash a torrent of semi-pornographic adverts. Yet pop ups are easily blocked and in some instances they do serve a purpose. They're like a conscience, reminding you of places you probably shouldn't have visited. Instead of a blonde turning up on your doorstep nine months later pushing a pram, you simply get a pop up. Seems like a reasonable deal. Pop ups keep you on your toes, they make a nice clicking sound, and they're also quite handy if you are actively looking for a date with a pneumatic woman of Eastern European origin.

JOHN PRESCOTT

He's fat, he's round, he dragged Labour down. But he packs a mean punch and he knows how to use a croquet mallet. So leave him alone. Now.

PRESIDENTIAL RALLIES

US Presidential election rallies combine the spectacle of an Olympic opening ceremony with the rhetoric of the Spanish Inquisition and the enthusiasm of an Osmonds concert circa 1973. The sight of thousands of middle-aged Republican or Democrat supporters behaving like high-school cheerleaders is truly something to behold. They parade placards declaring their undying love for their hero, except that, instead of Donny, it's George W. Bush, and, instead of Little Jimmy, it's Al Gore. They whoop and holler to order in a manner not seen since America last won the Ryder Cup, and if their candidate happens to mention the phrase 'tax cuts', you almost expect an outbreak of unbridled, joyous screaming, with Florida matrons storming the stage in the hope of grasping

Dubya's hand, or his mind, whichever of the two happens to be operating that day. To most sane people, the prospect of sitting through a DVD box-set of 'Ming' Campbell's greatest speeches or spending the night in an igloo with a hungry polar bear is eminently preferable to attending a US Presidential election rally.

But the good thing about these carefully orchestrated, saccharine-sweet rallies is that they immediately make us grateful for our own British politicians. Given the appeal of most of our MPs, this is no mean achievement. We just

don't appreciate razzamatazz. The only time we tried it – in 1992 when poor Neil Kinnock took to the stage triumphantly at Sheffield like an ageing rock star, punching the air and shouting 'well, all right, well, all right' – proved an unmitigated disaster. To show it didn't think much of his American-style antics, the British public ignored Kinnock at the polls in favour of Mr Grey, John Major. Of course, had we known that Major had been knocking off Edwina Currie for years, it would indeed have been all right for Kinnock, who would surely have won in a landslide. Our equivalent of the Presidential rally is the party conference, but it is like comparing a stag night to an afternoon tea dance. Polite applause is the norm at Blackpool, Scarborough or Brighton . . . and then only from those that are still awake. Any standing ovation is merely to offset the risk of DVT.

So as long as there are American politicians with their attendant worshippers, our lot seem bearable. Well, almost.

PROLONGED PAUSES

It all started with Ant and Dec. And now every presenter about to announce a winner or an eviction from a reality TV show has to insert an exaggerated pause – sometimes as long as twenty seconds – before declaring the result. Kate Thornton, Tess Daly, Cat Deeley, they all do it, supposedly to crank up the tension. My concern is that returning officers at the next general election will start doing it, which will drag proceedings on into the following week. Or that the practice will become de rigueur at the Oscars, ceasing only when some wannabe Hollywood starlet hyperventilates and collapses, unable to bear the tension any longer. Although these manufactured pauses are annoying, there is one thing you can do during them that will make you feel much better about yourself and indeed about life in general: switch off the bloody TV.

Q

QUEUING

Nobody queues like the British. We only have to see a sign saying 'Queue Here' and we immediately form an orderly line without actually knowing what we're queuing for. The reason the British army were routed by the Zulus in the nineteenth century was that our soldiers were dismayed to

see the enemy storming over the hill en masse instead of in a neat single file. As a country we may tolerate rapists, religious fanatics and murderers, but there is no place for queue jumpers.

Other nations mock us for our queuing fetish but at least it's better than an unruly free-for-all. Queuing is good for the soul – if not your soles – and can lead to lasting friendships. Total strangers meeting at the end of a supermarket queue have become engaged to be married by the time it has reached the checkout on a busy Friday evening. Queuing is based on the British sense of fair play, which rules that the early bird deserves to catch the worm rather than be reduced to a pile of feathers in a fight with other hungry birds. Along with Sunday roast lunch, the Trooping of the Colour and Sir Cliff Richard, queuing is part of our culture and, like Sir Cliff, it must be preserved at all costs.

R

RADIOHEAD

Radiohead are often labelled the gloomiest band in the world and lead singer Thom Yorke has been branded 'a miserable ginger dwarf'. So what? Rock music thrives on misery. There were all those songs about death in the Fifties, not to mention Leonard Cohen whose music made you feel, in the words of one reviewer, as if your dog had just died. And The Manic Street Preachers aren't exactly a bundle of laughs either. The best music comes from grief. Chirpy boy-bands merely cause grief.

RAP MUSIC

The great thing about rap music is when you hear it on the radio, you never have to think about which station you're on: you know immediately it's the wrong one.

RATS

Rats were invented by the PR man for mice. Everyone used to be scared stiff of mice with the result that thousands were beaten to death every year. But then rats took all the heat off mice. They were bigger and supposedly nastier. Suddenly mice weren't so bad after all; they were being kept as pets and were invited by Walt Disney to spearhead a new series of cartoon films, a job that would probably otherwise have gone to a cat or a dog. Rats had no chance. Even Ratty in *Wind in the Willows* was really a vole.

Rats have a right to feel aggrieved about their reputation. Scientists have since discovered that rats are highly intelligent, playful and actually quite clean, although living in sewers and being responsible for the spread of the Black Death do little to support that particular theory. As for the Pied Piper of Hamelin, rats see him as nothing but a mass murderer, the Boston Strangler of the rodent world. By contrast, in Hindu mythology rats are viewed as holy creatures. The rat is also one of the

twelve animals in the Chinese Zodiac. People born in the year of the rat are expected to possess qualities associated with rats, namely creativity, honesty, generosity and ambition. There's quick temper and wastefulness too, but nobody's perfect. And no mention at all of spreading disease. I bet rats weren't even to blame for the Black Death – it was probably mice in baggy jumpers.

REFEREES

Being a football referee is about as thankless a task as being Shane McGowan's orthodontist. Match officials have been shot, they have been stabbed, they have been run over, which, to most right-thinking people, appears a heavy price to pay for getting the offside rule wrong. This intimidation is not confined to minor football. There have been two high-profile cases in recent years. Swedish official Anders Frisk was forced into early retirement after receiving death threats following a controversial Champions League tie between Barcelona and Chelsea. And when Swiss referee Urs Meier disallowed a Sol Campbell goal for England against Portugal in a Euro 2004 quarter-final, he was sent 16,000 abusive e-mails (many describing him as a 'Swiss banker') and numerous death threats after British tabloids helpfully published his personal details. As a result he had to be placed under police protection. He went into hiding for a while and couldn't see his own children for four days. And all because England eventually went out of the tournament. That they did so on penalties – and that Mr Meier was not among the overpaid prima donnas who couldn't hit the back of the net from twelve yards – was evidently lost on the England fans.

Referees and their assistants have grown wearily accustomed to having their parentage, eyesight and honesty questioned on a daily basis, by supporters, players and managers alike. Sadly, it goes with the territory. Although German referee Robert Hoyzer caused a national scandal when he admitted being paid to fix games, the vast majority of referees are scrupulously honest. So for players, many of whom dive routinely in a bid to con the officials, to accuse those same people of cheating is a bit rich, which, of course, is exactly what today's Premiership stars are.

Usually the only time anyone stands up for the poor old ref is to get a better aim at him. But it's high time we were more tolerant towards match officials. We don't have to love them, send them Christmas cards, or pat their guide dogs, but we should respect their authority and recognise the fact that even Graham Poll (he of the three-card trick) is probably only human. Just think what would happen if we didn't have referees and everyone was simply allowed to get on with it? Players would brawl on the pitch, swear constantly and feign injury, while on the touchline managers would argue about the legality of every goal and start pushing and shoving each other. That would never do.

RINGTONES

Mobile-phone ringtones might be annoying to some people – particularly on public transport – but at least they drown out the sound of women talking about their operations and men relocating their catarrh. In fact, a chorus of ringtones unleashed simultaneously can sound every bit as tuneful as one of those wretched operatic groups that spring up every Christmas. The only reason anyone can have for objecting to a ringtone is if it's a particularly naff tune like 'Colonel Bogey' or 'Tie a Yellow Ribbon'. Therefore the key to success is to select the right tune, preferably something you can identify with, that relates to your occupation, personality or status in life. Someone working on a telephone switchboard might choose 'Smooth Operator', a parking attendant might opt for 'Chasing Cars', someone of a nervous disposition might pick 'Paranoid', and someone who's just been sacked from his job as a postman might go for 'Where The Streets Have No Name'.

ROYAL FAMILY

At around £30 million pounds a year, the British royal family doesn't come cheap. But when you consider that just the first eleven days of the war in Iraq cost Britain £90 million and that the United States has so far spent well over £250 billion on the Iraq war, the Queen suddenly seems like quite a bargain. Nevertheless, some people have the audacity to accuse the royals of being profligate, out-of-touch with reality, rude, and even lazy.

The Prince of Wales has been dismissed as a loony ever since he admitted talking to his plants. What his critics fail to recognise is that this was ideal preparation for his future conversations with Camilla. Recently it emerged that Charles required the services of a valet to squeeze toothpaste onto his toothbrush. But if Charles had done it himself, he might have made a mess of his clothes and anyway you can't expect a chap to squeeze his own toothpaste when he has a heavy day ahead, doing whatever he does. And it's not as if the valet also wipes the royal arse. Is it? Is it? Sources also claim that Charles instructs his staff to boil seven eggs in the morning, ranging from runny to rock hard so that he can choose which one he wants to eat. That sounds like perfectly reasonable behaviour. Any heir to the throne with a total disregard for money would do the same.

Meanwhile, the Duchess of Cornwall has been labelled 'monumentally lazy' after it was revealed that she undertook only 230 engagements in one year. But why should she suddenly start working her fingers to the bone? It's against her nature. No one wants to see her anyway.

The Duke of York has been nicknamed 'Air Miles Andy' by the same gutter press who would fawn all over him for an exclusive interview. And why? Because he spent £11,000 on a private flight from the Isle of Man to a golf function in St Andrews and another £6,000 on hiring a helicopter to fly seventeen miles to an air show. So he likes flying. Where would we be if a similar attitude had been adopted towards the Wright brothers? Besides, with the state of Britain's public transport network, you could hardly expect HRH to hop on a train when lunch was waiting. He would have been lucky to make the after-dinner mints. And a black cab would almost certainly have worked out even more expensive than the helicopter. Also it doesn't suit him to mix with the riff-raff. Look what happened in 2005 when Sydney airport staff wanted to submit him to a security check in the wake of worldwide terrorist attacks. Naturally he refused at first. They were probably republicans anyway.

Of course his father, the Duke of Edinburgh, is no stranger to controversy. On a tour of China, he once referred to the locals as having 'slitty eyes'. Slip of the tongue. He actually meant 'shitty pies'. Could have happened to anyone. In 1993 he told a Briton living in Hungary: 'You can't have been here long. You've not got a pot belly.' Slip of the tongue. He meant 'Pot Noodle'. Could have happened to anyone. He has been involved in other misunderstandings but they were all slips of the tongue. Could have happened to anyone.

Those who continually criticise the British monarchy should think what state the country would be in without a royal family:

- There would be no Royal Variety Performance, thus causing enormous hardship to legions of Eastern European jugglers and acrobats.
- Dozens of gay men would be unemployed.

- Helpless corgis would be slaughtered.
- Elizabeth and Philip would have to go into sheltered accommodation.
- Buckingham Palace would become a Starbucks.
- The Crown Jewels would be auctioned off on *Cash in the Attic*.
- Paul Burrell would never write another book.
- President Brown.

ROYAL MAIL

Once upon a time Britain's postal service was the envy of the world. There were up to five deliveries a day in some areas, regular collections, and a first-class stamp ensured next-day delivery. Then, gradually, the service fell into decline, to the extent that the Royal Mail changed the name of its Post Office subsidiary to Consignia in the hope that nobody would know who was to blame. Millions of pounds were spent on the re-branding but the new name proved so unpopular that just two years later millions more had to be spent on changing the name back to Royal Mail.

In 2004, the Royal Mail announced that as part of a revision of strategy (a popular euphemism for a cost-cutting exercise), it was phasing out the second daily delivery of post. To which, a chorus of householders across the UK asked: 'What second delivery?' Apart from a man in Bridgewater who claimed to have spotted a postman on a bicycle making a second, late-morning call, nobody had seen a second delivery in years, not since Darren Day was a virgin. In effect, it is not the second delivery that the

Royal Mail has abolished but the first delivery. Whereas the first post used to be delivered around breakfast time, now it doesn't appear until midday or sometimes as late as four o'clock in the afternoon – and that's in urban areas. In rural regions, it depends what time the pigeon can make it. Nor is a first-class stamp any longer a guarantee of next-day delivery (for that you have to pay a hefty Special Delivery charge at the Post Office). As for a second-class letter, you might as well throw it in the gutter. The chances of it being delivered to its destination are on a par with a Shetland pony's prospects of winning the Grand National.

The number of collections has also been drastically reduced. The collection time is so early in many places – preceding the delivery by several hours – that it is now impossible to reply by return of post. The collection time at 19,000 UK post boxes has been quietly brought forward to early morning – 6.30 a.m. in some places – as a result of which people have to post letters the night before. These early collections are designed to make it easier for the Royal Mail to hit its delivery targets – a policy in which customers act as nothing more than a minor irritant.

Not surprisingly, the Royal Mail has been accused of offering a second-class service for first-class prices. In 2006, it was fined £9.62 million for losing mail following the publication of figures which revealed that 15 million letters and parcels are lost, stolen or damaged in the UK every year. A report by MPs concluded that the Royal Mail is 'failing customers', adding that the postal service is 'chronically poor' in some areas.

But the Royal Mail is great and is doing a great job. Who

says so? The Royal Mail, of course. A spokesman haughtily dismissed the MPs' report, saying: 'It is absolute nonsense to suggest anything other than the Royal Mail's quality of service is at record levels. Its performance is among the very best in Europe and its prices are among the very lowest.' So there you are – our postal service is every bit as good as Moldova's. Regarding criticisms about late deliveries, the Royal Mail insists it is under no legal obligation to deliver to households before 9.30 a.m. but says it tries to make deliveries by midday . . . unless it has got something better to do. In fact, the Royal Mail is so pleased with itself that in December it decided to send a letter to all homes and businesses in the UK detailing its successes. But it hasn't arrived yet.

RUBIK'S CUBE

Did you ever think those people who appeared on TV to demonstrate how fast they could solve a Rubik's Cube puzzle were sad, pathetic nerds with no grip on reality, no concept of irony, and who desperately needed to get a life? Me neither.

RUDDY DUCKS

The North American ruddy duck is a cute little bird. With its pert upturned tail, it looks like something you put in the bath or one of those fairground plastic ducks you try to hook in the hope of winning a piece of cheap tat. Unfortunately, through no fault of its own, the ruddy duck is now seen as public enemy number one in some quarters. As a result of escapes from wildfowl collections, the ruddy duck rapidly established itself in Britain, from where it spread into Europe and threatened to wipe out the endangered native white-headed duck. For the ruddy duck is also a randy duck. It chases after anything in feathers and is more than happy to mate with the white-headed duck. Consequently the government has decided to eradicate the ruddy duck from the UK in a bid to save the white-headed duck from extinction.

But is it fair to blame the poor ruddy duck? While reluctantly supporting the cull, The Royal Society for the Protection of Birds acknowledges that the ruddy ducks are only doing what comes naturally to them. The ruddy duck can't help being sexually voracious, able to keep going all ruddy night. Maybe it could be brainwashed into believing that the white-headed duck is an avian Ann Widdecombe, thus eliminating instantly any risk of crossbreeding. Alternatively, the white-headed duck could be educated to put it about a bit more. The males could try buying the females flowers, taking them to dinner, quacking open a bottle of champagne, anything to raise the population. Or how about producing *A Good Sex Guide For Ducks*, but not making it available to ruddy ducks? They seem to know it all anyway.

Imagine the outcry if human sex machines were treated the same way as the ruddy duck, and the government announced a cull of Tom Jones, Rod Stewart and Mick Jagger. Now there's a thought.

DONALD RUMSFELD
Only joking.

S

SCAMPI

What exactly is scampi? Has anybody ever seen one swimming around in an aquarium or being hauled ashore in a trawlerman's net? Apparently it's supposed to be Norway lobster but in the UK just about any old shellfish is used as scampi. For all its mystery, scampi tastes undeniably good, and sometimes it's best not to know what you're eating. The first person that tasted an egg surely had no idea where it came from, otherwise he'd have been sick on the spot. Food snobs screw their noses up at scampi, remembering it as a staple diet of seventies' cuisine, but give me a decent plate of scampi in breadcrumbs rather than any poncey dish that contains the word *jus*.

SEAGULLS

OK, so they're vicious bastards with beadier eyes than Mr Burns, but along with candyfloss, cheap beer, and psychotic landladies, the sound of seagulls epitomises the

seaside. Also, it's quite entertaining to watch them mob yappy Pekinese and then crap over the owners.

SERIAL KILLERS

The general consensus of opinion seems to be that serial killers are not good. But think how much joy they would bring by reducing the population of tax inspectors, politicians, football agents, media consultants, children's-TV presenters, spin doctors, style gurus, market researchers, and Ben Elton.

SHOPPING CHANNELS

The appeal of TV shopping channels has remained a mystery to most of the population. QVC's most popular product is Diamonique, a diamond simulant, i.e. fake. We're talking leatherette here. Another channel sells beauty products endorsed by Joan Rivers. Who the hell would want to look like Joan Rivers? Even Shrek would baulk at looking like Joan Rivers. They might as well be selling hair care by Bruce Forsyth, lip gloss by Cherie Blair or skin cream by a Komodo dragon.

But mock ye not. In 2004, QVC's sales revenue in the US exceeded £2 billion and in the UK totalled £265 million, so someone must be buying must-have items, such as the weight loss patches that you put on the bottom of your feet, which are supposed to draw out the fat while you sleep! Apparently the royal family use home-shopping channels, buying 'functional stuff' such as crockery, kitchen gadgets and home cinema projectors. So if it's good enough for them . . . Shopping channels also supply a valuable service to the entertainment industry in that they provide jobs for presenters who aren't good enough to get work on hospital radio. Similarly, the channels offer excellent training for those hoping to progress to much higher things – such as game-show hostesses – by teaching presenters how to wax lyrical about a potato peeler. The ingenuity required to dream up fresh adjectives to describe a rotating clothes line is not to be scoffed at. Above all, with twenty-four-hour broadcasting, shopping channels provide an essential outlet for the elderly, the infirm and the terminally lazy.

SLEEPWALKING

Sleepwalking can take you to places you'd only normally visit in your dreams. A sleepwalking teenager was found perched precariously on the arm of a crane 130 feet above London; a woman discovered her sleepwalking husband mowing the lawn, naked; and in Australia an apparently respectable middle-aged woman used to leave the house while she was sleepwalking and have sex with complete strangers. Her double life only came to light when her partner, finding condoms scattered mysteriously around the house, became suspicious and caught her in the act one night. That's the great thing about sleepwalking – you can use it to excuse all types of outrageous behaviour. You only to have to look at this list of famous sleepwalkers:

- Vlad the Impaler
- Lee Harvey Oswald
- Lady Godiva
- Bill Clinton
- Dick Turpin
- Harry Houdini
- The Hound of the Baskervilles

SMALL TALK

Making conversation with complete strangers at social functions is widely acknowledged as one of the most difficult arts to master. Do you really want to hear about someone else's boring job, collection of golf tees or experiences in Morecambe? The trick is to lob in a couple of non sequiturs of your own. For example:

STRANGER: I'm in effluence. What about you?

YOU: Really? Did you know that grasshoppers can only hop if their body temperature exceeds 62 degrees Fahrenheit?

STRANGER: We've just appointed a new head of Human Resources.

YOU: Amazing. I bet you didn't know that Tonga once issued a postage stamp in the shape of a banana?

At this point you swiftly move on to the next person, leaving the stranger wanting more and thinking how thoroughly fascinating you are. Working the room at speed not only gives you a better chance of eventually stumbling across somebody remotely interesting, it also confuses the waiters who will repeatedly top up your glass and offer you extra vol-au-vents. Therefore a degree in small talk is an invaluable qualification and it can be yours provided you obey the following rules:

- Always appear gripped by the conversation, even if you're secretly thinking about whether or not you need to buy dishwasher tablets tomorrow.
- Never yawn.
- Never call anyone a boring old fart.
- Never eat chicken wings immediately before shaking hands with anybody important.
- Steer clear of innuendo. It will stick out a mile.
- Even in moments of sheer frustration, never poke anyone in the eye with a cocktail stick.

SOAP ON A ROPE

Not until Saddam Hussein has anything looked as good on the end of a rope as a bar of soap. Whose idea was it to put soap on a rope? Probably the same person who thought chicken was suited to a basket or that the ideal place for a ship was in a bottle. Along with television, the airplane and the Internet, soap on a rope was one of the great inventions of the twentieth century. Although after a few uses the soap would become horribly congealed on the rope and after a month you'd need a pickaxe to remove the excess sediment, the joy of the device was location, location, location. With the rope attachment, there was never any problem locating the soap in the bath. No need to hunt under rubber ducks or aircraft carriers. Soap on a rope was almost impossible to lose, particularly the popular 'Enery's 'Ammer, the shape of Henry Cooper's boxing glove in 'the great smell of Brut'. Not only did it last for several years, but also the bright red colour made it (and anything that came into contact with it, including skin) glow with a ferocity usually only achieved by nuclear reactors. Its distinctive scent also ensured that it was instantly detectable across entire continents. The brilliant concept of soap on a rope could easily be applied to other items that are wont to stray. So why not use a length of rope to tether ballpoint pens? Or paper clips? Or husbands?

SPAM

Armies have marched on Spam, Monty Python have sung about Spam, so can it really be that unpalatable? A six-year-old Dorset boy certainly didn't think so. He became so addicted to Spam that he ate his way through six tins of the stuff every week for three years and had to be sent to a child psychiatrist to get him back on a normal diet. I have fond memories of Spam. It was the picnic food of choice in the 1950s, before smoked salmon and the like became readily available. It was meaty, reasonably tasty in a Spammy sort of way, it filled a gap and it wasn't a hard-boiled egg. Therein lies Spam's image problem: it is still seen as a child of post-war rationing. People ate Spam because there was nothing much else around. The makers have tried to make it trendy again via a heavy advertising campaign suggesting that Spam fritters would make an ideal anniversary meal. Maybe that is Spam's future – as a marriage gauge. Because any modern marriage that can withstand Spam fritters as a wedding anniversary treat must be rock solid.

SPEED BUMPS

Traffic-calming devices have spectacularly failed to have a calming influence on drivers. Nevertheless, their manufacture has brought much-needed prosperity to a small Yorkshire town where the only other factory makes Coronation mugs. They also serve as excellent practice ramps for aspiring skateboarders, although BMX stunt riders have expressed disappointment at the degree of elevation obtained from a speed bump. However, the prospect of being mown down by an oncoming bus does provide a compensatory thrill factor.

SPORTS PSYCHOLOGISTS

Ben Crenshaw once reckoned he was about five inches from being an outstanding golfer, explaining 'that's the distance my left ear is from my right'. So much of sport is in the mind, although positive thinking can work in all walks of life. Noel Edmonds says that it resurrected his TV career. He wanted to be back on primetime television and his positive thinking worked, but sadly not for the rest of us who wished exactly the opposite. Much of Muhammad Ali's success was down to his supreme self-confidence and the demoralising effect it had on his opponents. Frankie Dettori is a great jockey partly because of his irrepressible belief in his own ability. On the other hand, footballer Emile Heskey has struggled to attain that level of sporting excellence, not necessarily because he lacks confidence but largely because he is shite.

If a psychologist can get inside a footballer's head, it must be a positive step and at least there is plenty of empty space there in which to operate.

'So repeat after me, we will win the World Cup, we will win the World Cup.'

'Thank you, Mr McClaren. Time for your medication.'

SUDOKU

Sudoku exercises your brain cells, it is a harmless way of passing several hours while waiting for train/plane/Godot, and it imbues you with a certain intellectual gravitas that you just don't get from playing Crash Bandicoot III.

SUPERMARKET TROLLEYS

The term 'off her trolley' could very well have stemmed from the first woman who attempted to steer a shopping cart on wheels around a supermarket. In the UK alone, more than 8,000 people are treated every year for injuries caused by supermarket trolleys. In South Wales in 2006, an eighty-year-old man was killed after joyriding in a trolley. In a scene like something out of *Last of the Summer Wine*, he charged down the supermarket aisle riding on the rear of the trolley shooting 'wheeeeee!' as his friend waited to pay. Unfortunately, the trolley overturned and the sprightly pensioner suffered a fractured skull. According to an acquaintance, his behaviour was by no means out of character.

Meanwhile, an Austrian supermarket introduced talking trolleys that pointed out bargains to shoppers, but the scheme was dropped following myriad expressions of customer dissatisfaction, some of which involved the use of a chainsaw. It was hardly surprising. Most people don't want to be lectured by a lump of erratic metal; all they demand from their supermarket trolley is that it moves in a straight line. But in doing so, they are guilty of rejecting the supermarket trolley's finest trait – eccentricity.

The weekly supermarket shop can be a tedious, soul-destroying experience, but pushing a trolley where all four wheels head in different directions simultaneously presents a thrilling challenge. It is the equivalent of riding a bucking bronco around the course at the Horse of the Year Show. All manner of contraptions and devices are capable of operating in a boring straight line but only a supermarket trolley possesses Mark Thatcher's qualities of navigation. You never know where it's going to take you. A supermarket trolley can help you meet new friends, just by steering itself into someone else's untamed cart. You can go into a supermarket with the intention of buying a joint of beef and emerge a committed vegetarian, simply because your trolley wouldn't let you anywhere near the meat section.

Detractors maintain that anything lacking the ability to walk straight must be of extremely low intelligence, but they've probably never had the courage to say that to a Scotsman on Hogmanay. On the contrary, I firmly believe that supermarket trolleys are far cleverer than we give them credit for. It can take a human being ages to get out of a supermarket car park, yet look how many trolleys manage to escape, even though they're supposed to be chained together. We often find them miles from home, enjoying a dip in rivers, sitting in people's front gardens or just loitering outside pubs. There is clearly far more to supermarket trolleys than meets the eye. Underestimate them at your peril.

SWEARING

Some say swearing is the root of all evil. Is it, bollocks!

SYNCHRONISED SWIMMING

It's a fair bet to say that whoever devised ballet never intended it to be performed underwater. You can't help thinking that Rudolf Nureyev's style would have been cramped somewhat by having to wear a snorkel, wetsuit and flippers. Yet underwater ballet pretty much sums up synchronised swimming, which should be no more an Olympic sport than tiddlywinks or gardening. While accepting that it's not exactly a sport for adrenalin junkies, at least it hasn't been soured by drugs allegations. Nor have there been any known fatalities, although interestingly, if one synchronised swimmer drowned, would the rest have to drown too? And it's really no worse than watching rhythmic gymnastics or dressage.

T

TATTOOS

A tattoo can say a lot about someone. Usually it says 'I got pissed once.' Although, on reflection, Jeremy Clarkson was ill advised to get a 'Sinclair C5' tattoo on his right shoulder and Paul McCartney probably regrets his 'Heather forever' tattoo, body artwork does have its advantages. For example, anyone whose face is covered in snake tattoos or a skull and crossbows is always likely to get a seat on a bus.

TAXI DRIVERS

Taxi drivers are much maligned, yet they provide a vital service throughout the world, always being willing to offer the weary traveller the benefit of their wisdom. In fact, so keen are they to share information that often they don't even wait to be asked.

- If you want to know what is wrong with the nation's economy, ask a taxi driver.
- If you want to know what is wrong with the nation's football team, ask a taxi driver.
- If you want to know what is wrong with the nation's youth, ask a taxi driver.
- If you want to know why the nation is going to the

dogs, ask a taxi driver.

- If you want to know where to go for your next holiday, ask a taxi driver.
- If you want to know why all other road users are idiots, ask a taxi driver.
- If you want to know who was sitting in the back of his cab the day before, ask a taxi driver.
- If you want to be parted with the contents of your wallet for a five-minute journey, ask a taxi driver.

TELEVISION EVANGELISTS

- In 1986, American TV evangelist Marvin Gorman was defrocked from his New Orleans ministry for 'immorality and conduct unbecoming to a minister' after he admitted to having had an extra-marital affair six years previously.
- In 1987, Assemblies of God minister Jim Bakker who, with his decorative wife Tammy Faye, had built up a money-spinning Christian theme park and a cable TV network with 13 million subscribers, was exposed as having committed adultery six years earlier with a twenty-one-year-old church secretary named Jessica Hahn. Bakker, leader of the Praise the Lord ministry, was forced to resign and aisle-wide views of Ms Hahn appeared in Playboy magazine.
- In 1988, Bible-thumping, self-appointed moral guardian Jimmy Swaggart, whose TV show reached over nine million US homes and was beamed to 140 countries, was defrocked after being caught on film

taking tattooed prostitute Debra Murphee to a New Orleans motel. He insisted that he had not had sex with the prostitute, but had paid her to perform pornographic acts. Ironically, Swaggart had helped orchestrate Gorman's downfall and had revelled in Bakker's demise, boasting: 'The only woman I ever kissed is my wife.' Swaggart begged forgiveness from his flock. In what turned out to be a reversal of a traditional Oscars speech of thanks, he confessed to his sins. Finally he said sorry to Jesus, 'the one who has saved me and washed me and cleansed me', but who had obviously missed a few bits with the flannel.

- In 1992, Jim Whittington, head of Fountain of Life Ministries, was jailed for ten years for fraud after widow Valeria Lust was coerced into donating her home to his ministry.

- In 2006, Pensacola, Florida, preacher Kent Hovind, founder of the Creation Science Evangelism Ministry, was found guilty on fifty-eight counts of tax fraud.

- In 2006, Colorado evangelist Ted Haggard (known as Pastor Ted) was forced to resign following allegations that he had taken drugs and had enjoyed a three-year affair with a male prostitute. Haggard had previously condemned homosexuality from the pulpit.

You can see a pattern emerging here: as a collective, American TV evangelists are about as honest, moral and trustworthy as the Jesse James Gang. Had they been around 2,000 years ago, they would have requested the Three Wise Men to bring gold, frankincense and a copy of *Knave*. They are porn-again Christians. Obviously – the lawyer has asked me to point out – this is a generalisation. Many TV evangelists are without a stain on their character, although in some cases, this is simply because they haven't been caught yet.

The world of TV evangelists may sound seedy, but in fact they perform a valuable service. It could be argued that anyone gullible enough to give them large donations is too stupid to be trusted to spend the money wisely anyway. And if by making sizeable contributions to ministry funds people become convinced that they will go to heaven, who is to deny them that comfort? It's no different from making jam for the harvest festival . . . just a little more draining on the wallet. Besides, these preachers, with their fire-and-brimstone delivery, are

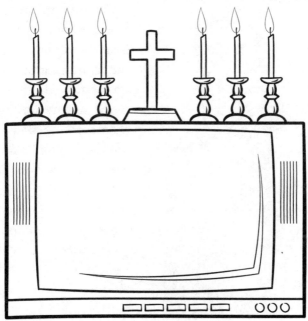

seriously entertaining. They make Ian Paisley sound like David Attenborough. If you can imagine Murray Walker conducting *Songs of Praise*, you'll get the picture.

TIPPING

Why do we tip in restaurants? It's as if good service is a bonus when it should be the norm. We are so conditioned to tipping that there are people rushed to hospital with food poisoning who still reach out from the stretcher to leave the waiter ten per cent before being loaded into the ambulance. Why do we tip taxi drivers for getting us from A to B in one piece? It's what they're supposed to do. Why

do we tip hairdressers? Is it in gratitude for emerging with both ears intact and for a haircut that doesn't look as if it has been done by a Black & Decker hedge strimmer? These people are supposed to be professionals for God's sake! As for fly tipping, ridiculous! What has a fly ever done to deserve a tip?

No matter how iniquitous tipping is – and really it is nothing more than a private stealth tax – withholding a tip or leaving a paltry amount can be immensely rewarding. Taxi drivers will mutter for England if you don't leave them a tip, but it is a good way of shutting them up. Waiters will slam the till receipt down on the table and confiscate the after-dinner mints. And madam can put her own bloody coat on! Hairdressers will vow to get even next time, in which case it's probably best to try a different establishment in future. With the exception of the likes of Michael Winner, the British are usually too polite to complain about lousy or even moderate service. We just want to escape. We don't want to make a scene. Therefore the best way of showing our displeasure is in the tip . . . or lack of it. That way, we can quietly register our protest without fear of being set upon by a crazed Polish chef brandishing a meat cleaver.

TOILET PAPER (SHINY)

Just as the red squirrel used to rule the roost until the grey invader took over, so shiny toilet paper was commonplace until soft Andrex and its cute puppies achieved a marketing coup. It may be unsatisfactory with a worrying tendency to smear, but at least you can take a comb out of your pocket, wrap over a sheet of shiny toilet paper and play a decent tune. Try the same with Andrex and you just end up with soggy pieces of tissue all over your mouth. And even on Cameron Diaz that's not an attractive look.

TRACTION (IN)

Lying in a hospital bed in traction can be deeply unsettling but look on the bright side: at least it's a chance to put your feet up for a while.

TRAINSPOTTERS

Trainspotting is the ultimate cheap hobby. All you need is a pencil, a notebook, a thermos, a round of cheese sandwiches, a camera (optional), a grubby anorak, either a beard or a pair of NHS glasses (if sporting both, you will be confused with a real-ale buff), and a thick skin to ward off all the abuse that will inevitably come your way. Unlike the rest of us, a long wait on a railway platform is never a disappointment for a trainspotter. For them, when a train pulls into a station and is unable to go any further because the driver has forgotten the way, it is the stuff of which dreams are made. It affords them the opportunity to inspect at close hand a Class 2 Meridian loco with Pentium processor and digital surround sound, or whatever it is. Trainspotters are friendly brethren, always eager to share their enthusiasm with any poor soul who happens to be passing. And they spend all day in the fresh air, broken only by the occasional whiff of stale armpits. It is true that they have one-track minds – they think *Points of View* is a programme about railway junctions – but the fact remains that there are an estimated 100,000 trainspotters in the UK, and even Michael Palin has been known to dabble. Can they all be wrong?

TRAVELODGES

People knock them, but they offer unparalleled views of car parks, power stations, flyovers and motorway junctions, and they're often located right next to a Little Chef. What more could anyone want?

TRIBUTE BANDS

In the entertainment hierarchy, tribute bands rank just below people who make funny shapes out of balloons. Yet so many leading acts have their own tribute band (The Bootleg Beatles, The Illegal Eagles, Bjorn Again) that it's the musical equivalent of having a stalker. And tribute bands do have some advantages over the real thing:

- They are cheaper to watch.
- They are only too happy to give autographs.
- They can carry on performing long after the original band has broken up.
- You don't get bombarded with their merchandise at a gig.
- The drummer is unlikely to die suddenly on stage.

And with so many new tribute acts springing up, it surely won't be long before we hear Unkeane, Razorlike, Antarctic Monkeys, 50 Pence Piece, Scissor Sisters-in-Law, Monophonics, Pulp Fiction, Frankie Goes to Chorleywood, and No Patrol.

TWITCHERS

Twitchers are the paramilitary wing of ornithologists. They will stop at nothing to catch a glimpse of a rare bird, travelling hundreds of miles, trampling over lawns and smashing down garden fences if necessary. Many home owners are scarred for life by an invasion from a marauding gang of twitchers: it's like being a doorman at Harrods on the first day of the January sales. Whilst their enthusiasm is admirable, twitchers frequently overstep the mark. After a rare rose-coloured starling landed in a Norfolk garden in 2006, twitchers hounded the exhausted bird so relentlessly for two days that eventually it didn't have the energy to escape the clutches of the neighbourhood cat. Twitching does sometimes go hand in hand with tragedy. In 2004, thousands of twitchers trailed

THE
ODDIE
BIRD

a disoriented American robin for two months until it settled on an industrial site in Grimsby. Just as they trained their expensive cameras on the rare visitor, a sparrowhawk swooped and ate it.

Even apart from their unbridled zeal, much is laudable about twitchers. For a start, as with trainspotters, there is the fellowship, the camaraderie. If a twitcher discovers a rare bird, he doesn't keep it to himself; he shares the news with as many people as possible. In how many other walks of life does such generosity of spirit prevail? Certainly not in commerce, sport, or vegetable growing, where every discovery is jealously guarded. A twitcher's life is an exciting one, similar in many respects to that of a secret agent. You never know when you're going to receive a call to travel halfway around the country – even the world – on a special mission. It's just that instead of a tuxedo and gun, your mode of attire is Barbour and binoculars. Indeed, it was a disappointment to many that Bill Oddie was overlooked in the search for the new James Bond. And twitchers aren't prone to some of the malaises that afflict modern society. They don't beat up their wives (except when the unfortunate spouse has happened to scare away a blue rock thrush), they don't go binge drinking for fear that it will impair their ability to focus, and they don't do drugs, unless you count the occasional packet of Swoop.

U

THE UGLY SISTERS

It's all too convenient to paint the Ugly Sisters as the villains of the piece in Cinderella. But look at things from their point of view. They had a younger stepsister foisted on them without any prior consultation or any consideration as to how the new arrival might upset the delicate balance of family life. While their strength lay in their personalities rather than their looks, their sister was undeniably beautiful. Who can blame them for being a mite envious, especially as Trinny and Susannah weren't

around to advise them on clothes to suit the fuller figure? The sisters faced a lifetime of being left on the shelf, hardly surprising since their feet were too big to fit into anything smaller than size 14 gumboots. They had no chance of finding happiness – and then to cap it all, the pretty sister gets off with a handsome prince. Some girls have all the luck! No, the Ugly Sisters weren't evil, they were tragically misunderstood heroines. Added to which, they've kept Christopher Biggins in work for decades.

ULAN BATOR

The Mongolian capital may be the coldest in the world and about as accessible as the works of Homer, but isolation does have its advantages. For a start, the locals don't have to worry about planeloads of drunken British tourists turning up in replica football shirts and declaring undying love to their goats. Nor are there busloads of happy-clappy Japanese visitors, armed with more cameras than you'd see on a paparazzi stakeout at Tom Cruise's house. And when it comes to TV travel-show reporters, they're more likely to receive a visit from Michael Palin than from Judith Chalmers, whose bright pink outfits would surely treble the number of incidents of desert blindness. The absence of tourists also means that the city's gift shops don't have to stock cute little models of Genghis Khan. Mongolia should keep its major city just the way it is: miles from anywhere. It should resist all overtures from easyJet and dismiss any plans to extend the Jubilee Line to Ulan Bator.

V

VEGANS

They may have boring diets and always look ill, but don't you just envy their farts?

VIBRATORS

Men convince themselves that vibrators are just a poor substitute for the real thing; but women know that it is men who are the poor substitute. Weigh up the evidence: a vibrator won't fall asleep on you, a vibrator can perform more than once a night without having to watch adult movies, you don't have to massage a vibrator's ego, a vibrator doesn't leave a mess on the bed, a vibrator doesn't want to go out drinking with its mates, a vibrator doesn't give a damn whether or not you've gained nine pounds, you don't have to make breakfast for a vibrator, and, above all, you know exactly where a vibrator has been. In fact about the only thing a man can do that a vibrator can't is mow the lawn.

VIRGIN TRAINS

Virgin Trains are viewed as the lepers of the UK rail network, but it is so unfair. People don't realise that,

thanks to Virgin, it is now possible to travel from London to Glasgow in under three days. They say the fares are expensive. Not so. You can buy a return ticket from London to Birmingham for less than the monthly repayment on a £100,000 mortgage. They say the fares system is complicated. Nonsense. Advanced Earlybird Apex Bransonbuster Off-Peak Supersaver Standard Returns are readily available on some routes except between 0630 hours and 2200 hours (not weekdays). They say the rolling stock is outdated. Utter garbage. Virgin's new Pendolino tilting trains give you that incomparable feeling of seasickness without ever having to leave dry land. You can sit back in your seat, relax, enjoy a cup of coffee and often catch it before it flies off the table. Anyway if you plan your journey carefully – i.e. stick to the east coast – you can travel for miles without going anywhere near a Virgin train.

VULTURES

They may not exactly be renowned for their fine plumage or chirpy disposition but vultures make excellent pets for a number of reasons:

- Visitors won't outstay their welcome.
- The whole family will be fitter because nobody dare sit still for long.
- The cat will finally realise who is boss.
- They are loyal and faithful in times of strife because they will never fly off while there's a whiff of sickness in the air.
- No one will ever fall asleep on the sofa again.
- They make good coathangers.
- You'll know straight away when Grandma dies.

But remember a vulture isn't just for Christmas. It will want to hang around at least until the funeral.

W

WAFER-THIN HAM

You used to be able to get a rasher of bacon or a slice of ham that made your plate groan under the sheer weight. But now when you go into a supermarket and buy a pack of thick bacon, it's no thicker than medium. And if you buy a pack of medium, the bacon inside is virtually transparent. At the very bottom of the porky food chain comes wafer-thin ham, designed solely as a sandwich filling. It is very popular with TV executives because it shares with them the trait of being completely devoid of taste. On the other hand, wafer-thin ham contains fewer calories than an amoeba, doesn't have any bony bits or fatty stuff that you expect to find in a proper animal, and you can eat ten slices without feeling at all greedy. Nauseous yes; greedy no. And at least it's not turkey ham. What the hell is turkey ham? I know Norfolk's known for its inbreeding, but what was Bernard Matthews thinking of when he first introduced a pig to a turkey? Come to think of it, what was the turkey thinking?

WASPS

Wasps are the psychopaths of the insect world. They sting you for a laugh, just because they can. But does that make them bad? After all, bookmakers sting you, but you don't go around trying to drown them in beer or swatting them with rolled-up newspapers. Not unless you've had a really bad run of luck. On the contrary, there is a lot we can learn from wasps. They have a strong work ethic, their queen doesn't cost the taxpayer a fortune, they get along together admirably, they kill garden pests, and they carry off that tricky combination of brown and yellow better than any supermodel.

WATER COMPANIES

At one stage in 2006, Thames Water was losing 196 million gallons of water a day through leaks. On the one hand, a drop in the ocean; on the other, enough to submerge Slough. So not all bad.

WEATHER WARNINGS

Nearly every day we are told that the Met Office has issued a severe weather warning about something or the other – a particularly blue sky, falling leaves in autumn, or a cloud formation that looks like a horse. All it needs is two drops of rain and the sandbags are out. Of course, it all dates back to Michael Fish and the 1987 hurricane when the weather forecasters were caught napping. Personally, I think the crop of weather warnings is just attention-seeking by the forecasters, but you can't blame them for trying to liven up their three minutes of air time in the absence of any typhoons or plagues of locusts. A

severe-weather warning guarantees the viewer's attention while Siân Lloyd sweeps her hand imperiously over the Brecon Beacons, and must provide a considerable boost to the ratings. So, if it keeps the forecasters happy and makes them feel important, battening down the hatches three times a week and attaching a ball and chain to your granny in case she gets blown away are a small price to pay.

WEEDS

The rule of thumb in distinguishing a weed from a flower is straightforward. If you put something in the ground and it dies, it's a flower; if it comes up year after year, it's a weed. However, in horticultural terms, the division between the two is much more blurred. Many of our favourite garden flowers are just cultivated versions of weeds. A weed is nothing worse than a plant whose virtues have yet to be discovered or one that simply comes up in the wrong place. So let's hear it for weeds. They are hardy, reliable, capable of resisting all known chemicals, and a number of weeds have medicinal properties. When was the last time you heard of anyone being cured by a rhododendron? And if it weren't for pulling out weeds on a regular basis, gardeners would get precious little exercise.

THE WELSH

Any country whose most popular comedian is Max Boyce deserves sympathy not hostility.

X

XMAS

Why do some people get so worked up about the word 'Xmas'? Sure it's an abbreviation, but so are hundreds of words in everyday usage. Do devotees of the Wellington boot get hot under the collar about the term 'wellie'? Traditionalists maintain that Xmas is all part of the steady dumbing down of Christmas, but it's hardly on a par with having the Virgin Mary portrayed as a single mother on benefits or having the Three Wise Men replaced by the Bethlehem Massive. Anyway Xmas fits more easily into a card, is a word that even the most feral youth can spell, and there's nothing else beginning with x that I can think of for this book.

Y

YOUTH HOSTELS

There are people who would rather milk rattlesnake venom than stay at a youth hostel. But youth hostelling can be an eye-opening experience – if only because you spend all night with your eyes open in case someone steals your wallet. Quite apart from the price, there are plenty more reasons for recommending the basic charms of a youth hostel.

- You can hear snoring in several different languages.
- You'll meet people who put the 'strange' into strangers.
- As a foreign backpacker, you will learn lots of new words and phrases such as 'fart', 'ten o'clock curfew', 'potato peeler' and 'indecent exposure'.
- You form an increasingly strong bond with your personal belongings.
- You realise what it must have been like living in a concentration camp.
- You appreciate home like never before.

YOUTUBE

Named the invention of 2006 by *Time* magazine, YouTube has taken the Internet by storm. YouTube is a positive Jamboree Bag of video clips, from foreign TV commercials and drunken celebrity rants to political bloopers and excruciating home videos of aunts behaving badly at weddings. Where else could you find a California real-estate agent offering a guided tour to a client's home alongside someone hand-farting 'The Star Spangled Banner'? Or an aspiring actor delivering an earnest Shakespeare audition next to a guy demonstrating the finer points of Spit Art?

In its short life, YouTube has already created some unlikely stars, none more so than Peter, a seventy-nine-year-old British grandfather. Using the name 'geriatric 1927', he has built up a devoted following for his 'Telling it all' series of posts, in which he warmly recalls his days as a radar mechanic during World War Two, and his time as a motorcycle salesman. YouTube has also been utilised by Canadian police to show clips of wanted criminals to an audience it would not normally reach via TV or newspapers.

YouTube is clearly capable of fulfilling a public service as well as providing an entertainment outlet but some have already labelled it the tool of the devil. It has been accused of encouraging violence after people filmed fights on mobile phones before uploading them on to YouTube. This 'Happy Slapping' lark is indeed a social problem and whoever dreamed it up deserves an unhappy slap, preferably delivered by one of those blokes who pull trains halfway across America with their teeth. But nobody called for mobile phones to be banned when Happy Slapping started. So why have a pop at YouTube?

No, YouTube is great. It gives the wonderful, the weird and the woeful a chance to express themselves in a manner not normally seen outside auditions for *The X Factor*. Above all, it is your platform. YouTube needs you.

Z

ZITS

A sure sign that your skin is not in immaculate condition is when Clearasil can only offer an estimate for treatment. And as a precaution friends advise that you only ever leave the house with a paper bag over your head. Yet whilst an outbreak of spots can be a curse, even zits have their bright points . . . usually just before you squeeze them.

- Blind people can read your face.
- Your face glows in the dark, which is especially useful when walking along country lanes at night.
- When you are asleep, friends can have hours of fun joining up the dots on your face to try and form the shape of an animal or bird.
- Market researchers never bother to stop you and ask whether you use whatever beauty product they are

promoting, because it is obvious from looking at your face that you don't.

- You'll always get work on *Crimewatch*.
- Along with a smooth Chablis and a full-body massage, squeezing a whitehead onto a mirror is one of life's great pleasures.

ZOOS

Zoos have acquired a bad image in recent times and have been replaced in many areas by safari parks, which give animals the freedom to roam and promise close encounters as if in the wild. But who wants to have a close encounter with a baboon's bottom through your car windscreen? And then you have to pretend to be having fun while watching a pack of them destroying your windscreen wipers. If these animals are so intelligent, why can't they be taught to do something useful, like change the oil? And then you get salivating lions eyeing up your car full of passengers and thinking: 'Mmmm, food. Wonder how you get it out of the tin?' With zoos, however, you can park your car in the car park and return to it later without the prospect of a £150 bill for monkey repairs. Once inside the zoo, you can stroll about safely with no risk of ending up as lunch. Zoos nearly always house a far greater variety of wildlife than safari parks and you only have to walk from one enclosure to the next to see it: you don't have to drive halfway round a county. Well-run zoos with spacious enclosures are educational, entertaining and valuable conservation tools. Anyway, where else are divorced dads supposed to take their kids for a couple of hours on a Sunday afternoon?

Zoos do vary in quality, and there are several telltale indicators that you're at a bad zoo:

- A sign says 'To the penguin'.
- The stripes on the zebra tend to peel away in the heat.
- The green mamba has a hoseclip attachment.
- The front half of the elephant goes in a different direction to the back half and says 'Ouch!' when you throw a bun at it. There is also a zip beneath its trunk.
- The chimpanzees have to prepare their own tea party.
- The camel has a detachable hump.
- The paint on the white tiger is still wet.
- The lion sits still all day and looks uncannily like Simba from *The Lion King*.
- It's the bear's day off.